Give God the Glory!

Know God and Do the Will of God
Concerning <u>Your</u> Life

STUDY GUIDE

Give God the Glory! Series
Other books in this series by Kevin Wayne Johnson

Know God and Do the Will of God Concerning <u>Your</u> Life
Book #1, © 2001
Fifth Printing
ISBN: 978-0-9705902-0-6
Price: $10.99

Called to be Light in the Workplace
Book #2, © 2003
Second Printing
ISBN: 978-0-9705902-1-3
Price: $14.95

Let Your Light So Shine, a devotional/gift book
Book #3, © 2004
Third Printing
ISBN: 978-0-9752572-9-6
Price: $7.95

The Godly Family Life
Book #4, © 2005
Second Printing
ISBN: 978-0-9705902-3-7
Price: $13.00

Your Role in Your Family, a devotional/gift book
Book #5, © 2006
First Printing
ISBN: 978-0-9705902-4-4
Price: $7.95

Give God the Glory! STUDY GUIDE
Know God and Do the Will of God Concerning <u>Your</u> Life
Book #6, © 2008
ISBN: 978-0-9705902-2-0
Price: $15.00

To order, visit our online stores at: <u>www.writingforthelord.com</u> / <u>www.writingforthelord.org</u>

Give God the Glory!

Know God and Do the Will of God Concerning Your Life

STUDY GUIDE

Kevin Wayne Johnson

Writing for the Lord
M I N I S T R I E S

www.writingforthelord.org / www.writingforthelord.com

Writing for the Lord Ministries, Clarksville, MD 21029
Kevin@writingforthelord.com (e-mail)
http://GiveGodtheGlory.wordpress.com (blog)
1 (443) 535-0475 (phone) / 1 (410) 340-8633 (cell)
Copyright © 2008 by Kevin Wayne Johnson
First Printing. Published 2008

ISBN: 978- 0-9705902-2-0

Library of Congress Catalog Number: 2008933087

Cover Concept by Kevin Wayne Johnson
Cover Design by The Mazzochi Group © 2001
Zendra Manley, Chief Executive Officer and Graphic Designer
Three Rivers, MI
1 (877) 842-6916

Edited by: Hallagen Ink
Tanya Brockett, MBA
Crozet, VA
1 (434) 409-7058

Distributed throughout the United States, Canada and internationally by:
　(1) STL Distribution of North America
　　　522 Princeton Drive
　　　Johnson City, TN 37601 USA
　　　1 (800) 289-2772
　　　1 (888) 785-2432 Stock Check
　　　www.stl-distribution.com
　(2) Black Christian Book Distributors, LLC
　　　8528 Davis Boulevard, Suite 134
　　　N. Richlands, TX 76180 USA
　　　1 (214) 764-4029
　　　www.BlackCBD.com

Unless otherwise noted, all scripture references within the text are taken from the King James Version of *The Holy Bible*, The New Open Bible Study Edition, Thomas Nelson, Incorporated, 1990. Other versions include the New International Version (NIV), Amplified Version (Amplified), Today's New International Version (TNIV), New Living Translation (NLT), New Century Version (NCV), the New King James Version (NKJV), and New International Reader's Version (NIRV), taken from BibleGateway.com. Extremely long passages are divided by unnumbered verse.

Attention colleges; universities; non-profits; hospitals; prisons; independent bookstores; regional, national, and international suppliers; corporations; civic organizations; churches/church bookstores; & publishers:

Quantity discounts are available for bulk purchases of this **Study Guide** for educational training purposes, fundraising, or gift giving. Special books, booklets, articles, or **Study Guide** excerpts can also be created to fit your specific needs.

For special quotes, information, or for answers to your questions, please contact the publisher or author.

Printed in the United States of America

This Study Guide is based on Book #1 in the series, **Give God the Glory!**
Know God and Do the Will of God Concerning <u>Your</u> Life
Here is what others around the country have to say about **Give God the Glory!**

"The author of **Give God the Glory!** is proof that God does work with and through people, as he observes in the introduction. There is honesty in this book that leads to the Word. I am grateful Deacon Kevin W. Johnson includes the Scriptures...as they reinforce the power in this book for new and 'retired' Christians."

—ChristianBookReviewer

"Congratulations on the publication; I wish you great success with your first printing. Your book, Kevin, touched me; please know our prayers are with you as well."

—Gayle King, *Editor-at- Large, "O" The Oprah Magazine, New York City*

"Every Christian is gifted and commissioned to faithfully administer the manifold grace of God. With such a high calling it is imperative that we live each precious moment with a precise revelation of our part in God's overall plan. Kevin Johnson's book, **Give God the Glory!** sets out to help the reader discover that revelation. His timely message is both practical and penetrating providing a comprehensible plan of action well worth implementation."

—Lawrence Powell, *Pastor, Agape Family Worship Center, Rahway, New Jersey*

"Give God the Glory! is full of in-depth information for the Christian and non-Christian alike. The author has done extensive research of the Holy Bible and various secular resources. Reading this book will provoke one to consider their purpose for living. You will be convinced, as I was, that the Word of God is true and applicable for living in the 21st century. I recommend *Give God the Glory!* as wonderful literary work to be included in your personal library."

—Reverend Melvin Johnson, Sr., *Pastor & Founder, True Disciple Ministries Bible Institute (an Evangelical Training Association-affiliated Institute), Somerville, New Jersey*

"Give God the Glory! is a how-to book. It takes the words of the Bible and applies them to life. This book will open the word to your day-to-day life. The author gives his interpretation, and a good one, of the word. Read, apply, and enjoy."

—William L. Rosser, Jr., *Rosser Family Dentistry (retired), Richmond, Virginia*

"Give God the Glory! offers useable information that can be referred to time and time again in your library. It covers diverse topics conducive to the enhancement of family relationships. This work is also easy to read and will prove to be enjoyable and enlightening. Johnson encourages his readers to 'Know God and Do the Will of God Concerning Your Life,' which is practical use of a most appropriate subtitle. He enthusiastically embraces God's word for his life and expresses it in a way that gives readers incentives to do the same."

—Purpose magazine, *Book Views, Columbus, Ohio*

"Reading this inspirational book is a life-changing experience. It is truly a blessing for all of us who wish to learn to follow God's plan in our lives. I recommend *Give God the Glory!* to anyone who is searching for a guide to a more fulfilling spiritual life. Through the special gift of his writing ministry, Kevin Johnson models for all of us the ways in which we can each use our own talents to bring others to the Lord and to spread the word of the gospel."

—**Nancy Boyd-Franklin, Ph.D.,** Professor, Rutgers University, Co-author with her husband,
Dr. A.J. Franklin, of the book, *Boys into Men: Raising Our African American Teenage Sons*

"Deacon Kevin W. Johnson gives us a successfully laid out strategy in helping us to *Give God the Glory!* He shares his personal testimony. He provides us with scriptural support and, through these pages, gives us the opportunity to look within ourselves and realize that God has been truly good to us and we *must* take the time, everyday of our lives, to give Him the Glory. He desires and deserves! I would also encourage anyone who wishes to have an impact on developing a deeper relationship with Jesus Christ, as well as introduce others to Christ, to read this book. I am proud of this first of many literary contributions Deacon Kevin will have the privilege to share with the World at large."

—**Patricia Webster,** Senior Pastor, Shiloh Pentecostal Church, Inc.,
Christian Love Center, Somerville, New Jersey

"When pondering the big question, 'What is the meaning of life,' some readers may find comfort and answers in *Give God the Glory!* a book written by ministry leader Kevin Wayne Johnson. *Give God the Glory!* includes scripture that reinforces the author's words with God's. Topics in the book are designed to be helpful to family situations and personal relationships. Within the six chapters of the book, there are specific instances to encourage readers to give a little bit of themselves everyday to God."

—*The Courier News,* A Gannett Newspaper serving Central Jersey, Bridgewater, New Jersey,
Sujata Parida, Staff Writer, November 21, 2001

"A wonderful book that helps the reader to view acts of faith in the author's life, which can be translated into strength and sustained faith for the reader. Kevin Wayne Johnson joyously embraces the words of God through the Bible and his acts of Christian faith. This book is a great book for those on a faith journey. It will strengthen their understanding of living a life of faith and expose what it truly means to *Give God the Glory!*

—**Dallas BET newspaper,** Valder Beebe, Wedding and Lifestyle Editor, December 20–26, 2001

"The language used in this book is descriptive, understandable, and clear. The author provides contextual information, references, and lots of easy to understand definitions. The book provides a blueprint of how to strengthen your Christian walk. One of my favorite parts of the book was the section that covered spiritual gifts. The book will have you grabbing pen and paper so that you can takes notes. It is thorough and inspiring. I am sure that if you read this book with an open heart and answer the questions to consider that the author has listed at the end of each chapter, you will be touched. This was an excellent book and I hope that Mr. Johnson continues his writing for the Lord."

—**Tee C. Royal,** Founder, Book Reviewer, R.A.W. SISTAZ book club

"Give God the Glory! is a literary blessing to all who will read it. Your book has such insight on God's personal relationship with us. This is a must read for those who want a devotional and spiritual uplift in the Holy Ghost. May God continue to inspire you to write so that many will be led to *Give God the Glory!"*

—**Reverend Ronald L. Owens,** Senior Pastor, New Hope Baptist Church, Metuchen, New Jersey

If any man speak, let him speak as the oracles of God; if any man minister, let him do it as of the ability which God giveth: **that God in all things may be glorified** *through Jesus Christ, to whom be praise and dominion for ever and ever. A-men.*

—1 Peter 4:11 KJV

Whoever speaks, [let him do it as one who utters] oracles of God; whoever renders service, [let him do it] as with the strength which God furnishes abundantly, so **that in all things God may be glorified** *through Jesus Christ (the Messiah). To Him be the glory and dominion forever and ever (through endless ages). Amen (so be it).*

—1 Peter 4:11 Amplified

Foundational Scripture (emphasis added)—*Writing for the Lord* Ministries, LLC

*The heavens declare the **glory of God**; and the firmament sheweth his handywork.*

—Psalm 19:1 KJV

*The heavens declare the **glory of God**; the skies proclaim the work of his hands.*

—Psalm 19:1 TNIV

IN LOVING MEMORY OF GRANNY

As I did with the initial book in this series, I dedicate this **Study Guide** to the loving memory of my maternal grandmother, Granny. She was a God-fearing woman who professed that I would grow up to be a preacher when I was about eight years old as she touched me on my clean-shaven head one day in her home. It is a memory of her that I will never forget. I also vividly remember observing Granny on her knees praying to God consistently and persistently.

Thank you, Granny, for your Godly example.

CONTENTS

ACKNOWLEDGMENTS

First and foremost, I thank God, who, through His love for me, transferred me from the power of darkness into His marvelous light when I simply confessed Jesus Christ as my personal Lord and Savior. The gift of writing has been manifested in me, and revealed unto me, as a means to spread the gospel of Jesus Christ. I am eternally grateful for it.

I thank my lovely wife, Gail, who has added tremendously to my life. Thank you for your advice and consistent promotions. I love you more each year along with our three sons, Kevin, Christopher, and Cameron. Because of you, I look forward to each day as a husband, a father, and a man.

I thank my parents, Ernest and Adele, who led, guided, and directed me throughout my childhood, adolescent, and young adult years. Dad's military service in the U.S. Marine Corps instilled discipline and confidence in me during my early years that are paying dividends even today. Dad, your inspiring words, *"Be prepared,"* will be passed on to my sons. Mom's nurturing and diligent attendance in church taught me, as a boy, that God is real. While Dad was away in Vietnam and Okinawa, Japan, fighting in America's wars, Mom persistently kept me focused on the Lord through activities such as Sunday school and Vacation Bible School at Ebenezer Baptist Church in Richmond, VA.

I thank my former Pastor, Patricia Webster (Shiloh Pentecostal Church, Somerville, NJ) who confirmed the call that God has on my life. This book series was birthed under Pastor Pat's leadership. I also thank my current church family, Celebration Church, Columbia, MD, and my current pastor Robbie Davis for the encouragement, inspiration, and support as I write for the Lord. Thank you to my Christian brother Steve Gilliland, Chief Executive of Performance Plus in Pittsburgh, PA, who inspired and challenged me to write my first book during a training class in New York City on March 9, 2000.

Finally, I thank all family members and friends who have touched my life in a positive way. Your love and support have added enormously to my life and have helped to shape me into the person that I am today. For that, I thank you and love you all.

Glory!

A divine quality. Literally meaning heavy or weighty.

It represents the brightness, splendor, and radiance of God's presence as well as His visible revelation of Himself.

Our word 'doxology' comes from 'doxa,' the Greek word for Glory.

INTRODUCTION

The Lord gave the word: great was the company of those that published it.

—Psalm 68:11 KJV

The Lord gave a message. Many people made it widely known.

—Psalm 68:11 NIRV

*T*he ***Give God the Glory!*** series of books and devotionals is one of the many ways that I am personally able to glorify God—*through the blessed gift of writing.* ***Give God the Glory!*** is a *nine-book* series with a focus on putting God first and foremost in all that we do each day:

(1)   In our personal relationships,

(2)   In the workplace,

(3)   Within our family,

(4)   In the church, and

(5)   While at recreation.

Each main title is accompanied with a companion devotional and gift book.

This Study Guide is the culmination of numerous personal experiences and accounts as a member of the body of Christ. The pages contained herein comprise many years of personal Bible study, reading various texts and articles, and intent listening to powerful sermons that I have enjoyed. This Study Guide is an ideal resource for your church small groups, personal Bible study, pastors, church leaders, religious organizations, Bible students, book lovers, and readers.

This book is written to *all* of God's people. Regardless of one's personal religious belief(s), God's grace and mercy is sufficient to meet all of the needs of His people. I am convinced, by faith, that God's gift to us all—His only begotten Son, Jesus Christ—has redeemed us from the curse of the law, so that we may enjoy life, and enjoy it abundantly (John 10:10). For those who do not have a personal relationship with God, through Jesus Christ, it is my prayer that this Study Guide, as well as any of the ***Give God the Glory!*** series of books, will open all hearts and minds concerning God's love for us, be the spark that ignites a burning desire to know Him, and cause us to rely upon Him in **every** aspect of our lives.

Through the ***Give God the Glory!*** series of books, and this Study Guide in particular, my intent is to share my personal experiences with others, supported by scriptures throughout, as a member of the body of Christ, so that all of our readers may have the desire, courage and fortitude to spread the gospel of Jesus Christ.

OVERVIEW OF THIS STUDY GUIDE

All the commandments which I command thee this day shall ye observe to do, that ye may live, and multiply, and go in and possess the land which the LORD sware unto your fathers.

—Deuteronomy 8:1 KJV

Blessed is he that readeth, and they that hear the words of this prophecy, and keep those things which are written therein: for the time is at hand.

—Revelation 1:3 KJV

Studying the Bible is an incredible experience for all who desire to more clearly understand how God works with, and through, people. A person desiring to minister to others must understand how to develop the spiritual depth which comes from biblical knowledge. No book can substitute for studying the Bible itself, nor can the most capable person apply the Bible's message to another person's life. However, as expressed in the subtitle of this book, it is my goal to increase one's desire to "Know God and to Do the Will of God Concerning Your Life" based upon what God has revealed through my life.

Each chapter of **Give God the Glory!** begins with an *Old Testament* and a *New Testament* scripture (Chapter Three is the only exception). All scripture references are taken from the *King James Version* (KJV), the New International Version (NIV), Amplified Version (Amplified), Today's New International Version (TNIV), New Living Translation (NLT), New Century Version (NCV), the New King James Version (NKJV), and the New International Reader's Version (NIRV) of *The Holy Bible*. The purpose for referencing, or identifying, two passages of scripture is twofold:

1. To support one another, relative to the topic at hand, both before the birth of Christ (the law) and after Christ's death and resurrection (grace); and

2. To demonstrate the power of God's Word as revealed by at least two different writers of their respective time.

The following scriptures validate the strength of one's testimony whenever two or three witnesses are on one accord relative to the issue or topic at hand:

It is also written in your law, that the testimony of two men is true.

—John 8:17 KJV

In your own Law it is written that the testimony of two men is valid.

—John 8:17 NIV

One witness shall not rise up against a man for any iniquity, or for any sin, in any sin that he sinneth: at the mouth of two witnesses, or at the mouth of three witnesses, shall the matter be established.

—Deuteronomy 19:15 KJV

You must not convict anyone of a crime on the testimony of only one witness. The facts of the case must be established by the testimony of two or three witnesses.

—Deuteronomy 19:15 NLT

In the book of Matthew, for example, Jesus is quoted by Matthew, the tax collector, on the proper way to handle someone that offends you. In the Scripture, Jesus orchestrates a biblical example of how to gain a brother through humble confrontation. Initially, the matter should be handled one-on-one, between the offender and the offended. However, if the offender does not hear, then take with you two or three others for the purpose of humble confrontation. In this manner, the truth can be established in the presence of two or three witnesses. The scripture reads as follows:

But if he does not listen, take along with you one or two others, so that every word may be confirmed and upheld by the testimony of two or three witnesses.

—Matthew 18:16 Amplified

But if he will not hear thee, then take with thee one or two more, that in THE MOUTH OF TWO OR THREE WITNESSES EVERY WORD MAY BE ESTABLISHED.

—Matthew 18:16 KJV (emphasis added)

The overriding theme of this book is to **glorify God in all that we do so that we, in turn, will lead others to Christ**. The six chapters of this Study Guide contain a central theme. They are as follows:

PART I—KNOW GOD (*mental or attitudinal*)

To know God, means that we develop an intimate relationship with Him. In doing so, we:

- ✓ Glorify Him in all that we do, say, and think;
- ✓ Recognize and acknowledge our "calling"; and
- ✓ Use our spiritual gifts to maximize our productivity in the earth.

1. Chapter One—*Glorify God at all Times*
   Central Theme: Glorify God in words, thoughts, and deeds so that others will come to know Him.

   Our *lifestyle* is the key to glorifying God through words (spoken), thoughts (inner man & personality), and deeds (actions). It is our *lifestyle* (what others see) that is on display whereby others should observe "distinctively different" character traits that they not are accustomed to seeing everyday. In becoming "doers" of the Word of God, these character traits transcend our sin nature and are manifested in our desire to eradicate evil through good works.

2. Chapter Two—*You're Called (whether you know it or not)*
Central Theme: Recognize and acknowledge your calling.

Each of us is born with a Godly purpose to fulfill in this earth. Our Godly purpose cannot become a reality until we are first reconnected with the creator (God), through Jesus Christ. This first step, salvation, paves the way toward the recognition and acknowledgment of our assignment in the earth: To seek and to save those who were lost (Luke 19:10 & Matthew 18:11). How we each fulfill that respective assignment differs, yet the objective is the same: Love God, hate sin, and spread the gospel (good news!).

3. Chapter Three—*Knowing Your Spiritual Gift(s)*
Central Theme: Using your gift(s) to maximize your productivity.

God has established in our hearts certain gifts that are operational within the earth-realm. These twenty (20) gifts are categorized as power or protectional (operational), functional, and perfecting. These 20 gifts work in unison with the nine fruit of the Spirit (Galations 5:22–23). The Word of God operates through us, as predestined before the Earth was formed, based upon the gift(s) that God has entrusted us with. In order to be fully used by God, we must know and understand our gift(s) in order to maximize our productivity in the kingdom of God. In doing so, we also raise the level of productivity of those who are within our sphere of influence.

PART II—DO THE WILL OF GOD (*requires action*)

To do the will of God means that we:

- ✓ Spread the good news of Jesus Christ;
- ✓ Take hold of our covenant rights and benefits as believers; and
- ✓ Take on the role of a servant to be a blessing to others.

4. Chapter Four—*Spread the Gospel!*
Central Theme: Tell others about the good news of Jesus Christ.

Christians are compelled to tell and/or show others of the "good news" of Jesus Christ. We are commanded to do so, but there should be a yearning in the heart to do so nonetheless. This can be accomplished through our lifestyle, inviting others to church, and ministering to other's needs during a low point in their lives.

5. Chapter Five—*Stand tall by Knowing Your Covenant Rights*
Central Theme: Take hold of your covenant rights and benefits as a believer.

Throughout The Holy Bible, there are forty-four estimated recorded accounts that are prophesied by the writers of the Old Testament that are ultimately revealed in the New Testament. The Old Testament of the scriptures established "the law," that is, the Ten Commandments. Under the law, God pronounced his expectations for a Godly lifestyle, through Moses, to the people of that time. The New Testament of the scriptures, beginning with the book of Acts, establishes a new and revised last will and testament (covenant) of the Lord Jesus Christ, called "grace." We have been redeemed from the curse of the law, and transferred from the power of darkness into His marvelous light (1

Peter 2:9). Grace is God's omnipotent power working on behalf of the believer and our "Bill of Rights" is expressly revealed in the book of Romans through the book of Jude.

6. Chapter Six—*Be a Blessing to Others*
Central Theme: How to be a servant.

Service to others is essential within the Kingdom of God. Jesus walked the earth as a young child, adolescent, young man, and man, in preparation for His role as a servant. At the approximate age of 30, He actually took on the role of a servant throughout his three and one-half years of earthly ministry. Humbling ourselves as children and not thinking more highly of ourselves than we ought (Romans 12:3), serve as key barometers in our respective ministries. Whatever office you hold within your local church, service to others is the most important, and perhaps most misunderstood, aspect of the ministry.

This Study Guide reflects 15+ years of reading about diverse topics that are of extreme interest to me. As avid readers of a wide range of topics and interests, our personal growth and development relative to God's Word will be expanded by adding this Study Guide to your library. Each chapter concludes with five thought-provoking questions for your personal Bible study, devotion, and meditation time to draw closer to God. All references in this Study Guide are intended to add further verification that God's Word is preeminent in the earth, and that man only knows in part. Several references used will validate such. The message that I am attempting to convey throughout this Study Guide, coming in agreement with its overriding theme, is to encourage and challenge us to apply Godly knowledge, and practical application of the Word of God, to Give God the Glory for the things that he has done! In doing so, we will lead others to Christ; for it is correct biblical knowledge that will forever serve as a precursor for truth. This has been my personal experience.

Now, let's *Give God the Glory!*

Part I — KNOW GOD

*Thus saith the LORD, Let not the wise man glory in his wisdom, neither let the mighty man glory in his might, let not the rich man glory in his riches: But let him that glorieth glory in this, that he understandeth and **knoweth** me, that I am the LORD which exercise lovingkindness, judgment, and righteousness, in the earth: for in these things I delight, saith the LORD.*

—Jeremiah 9:23–24 KJV (emphasis added)

*Thus says the Lord: Let not the wise and skillful person glory and boast in his wisdom and skill; let not the mighty and powerful person glory and boast in his strength and power; let not the person who is rich [in physical gratification and earthly wealth] glory and boast in his [temporal satisfactions and earthly] riches; But let him who glories glory in this: that he understands and **knows** Me [personally and practically, directly discerning and recognizing My character], that I am the Lord, Who practices loving-kindness, judgment, and righteousness in the earth, for in these things I delight, says the Lord.*

—Jeremiah 9:23–24 Amplified (emphasis added)

Chapter One

Glorify God at all Times

Our *lifestyle* is the key to glorifying God through words (spoken), thoughts (inner man and personality), and deeds (actions). It is our *lifestyle* (what others see) that is on display whereby others should observe "distinctively different" character traits that they not are accustomed to seeing everyday. In becoming "doers" of the Word of God, these character traits transcend our sin nature and are manifested in our desire to eradicate evil through good works.

All nations whom thou hast made shall come and worship before thee, O Lord; and shall glorify thy name.

—Psalm 86:9 KJV

But we see Jesus, who was made a little lower than the angels for the suffering of death, crowned with glory and honour; that he by the grace of God should taste death for every man.

—Hebrews 2:9 KJV

*T*o know God is to *glorify* Him at all times. That is, in every aspect of our lives and with every inch of our being. Our lifestyle is viewed as either the magnet that draws people to an omnipotent God or turns them away. When our outward appearance manifests peace, joy, love, fulfillment, and contentment, all of which are possible with God, then others who are within our sphere of influence will desire to have those character traits manifested in their lives as well.

God is great and He is greatly to be praised! As we wake each morning, He is to be praised for allowing us to hear the alarm clock—that is if you need one. For it is not the sound of the alarm on the clock that awakens you and I, it is *hearing* the alarm. Similarly, obedience to the Word of God allows us to be sensitive to His voice. We hear God when He is speaking wisdom into our lives. Faith (the ability to know without seeing in the natural) comes by hearing. The more we hear God, and His Word, the stronger our faith in the things of God.

Knowing about God is fascinating. Knowing God personally is life changing. In this chapter, God sets forth many examples of how we can glorify Him day and night. God demonstrates in four ways how we can glorify Him at all times. They are through:

- ✓ The parables of Jesus—a look at Jesus' earthly example(s) relative to words, thoughts and deeds;
- ✓ Our human body—which is wonderfully and marvelously made;
- ✓ Our lifestyle—distinctively different character traits from the world; and
- ✓ Our faith—the *only* way to please God.

<u>Central Theme</u>: Glorify God in words, thoughts, and deeds so that others will come to know him.
<u>Keyword</u>: Glorify

"Glorify" defined:

Pā'ar (Old Testament)—is a verb and means "to glorify." It is used thirteen times in the biblical Hebrew.

Doxazō (New Testament)—means "to magnify, extol, praise." "To do honor to and to make glorious."

THE PARABLES OF JESUS

Many of us own a copy of *The Holy Bible*. Some of us may have many copies in different languages. This ancient book, written originally in Hebrew and Greek, with small portions in Aramaic, is still the most influential book in history, according to a 1996 survey of United States citizens. It is, by far, the overwhelming winner among influential books.

Jesus Christ used natural examples to extract spiritual meanings throughout the New Testament books of Matthew, Mark, and Luke. These natural examples are referred to as parables. It is derived from the Greek word *parabole,* which is a narrative or saying dealing with earthly things with a spiritual meaning. A parable is a noun and is a short allegorical (figurative) story designed to illustrate or teach some truth, religious principle, or moral lesson. It can be also referenced as a statement or comment that conveys a meaning indirectly by the use of comparison, analogy, or the like. No names are ever mentioned in the parables with the one exception of Lazarus, as found in Luke 16:19–31 (Parable of the Rich Man and Lazarus). More than half of the thirty-two parables that Jesus told in *The Holy Bible* had to do with money[1]. The others focused on children, parties, feasts, wineskins, and orchards.

In the book of Psalms, it was prophesied that God would communicate important messages to His people by the use of parables. Chapter 78 is one of two historical Psalms (105 is the other). In this chapter, God's continued guidance in spite of unbelief is the theme, yet He reminds Israel of His goodness:

Prophetic Scripture

I will open my mouth in a parable: I will utter dark sayings of old: Which we have heard and known, and our fathers have told us. We will not hide them from their children, shewing to the generation to come the praises of the LORD, and his strength, and his wonderful works that he hath done.

—Psalm 78:2–4 KJV

For I will speak to you in a parable. I will teach you hidden lessons from our past— stories we have heard and known, stories our ancestors handed down to us. We will not hide these truths from our children; we will tell the next generation about the glorious deeds of the LORD, about his power and his mighty wonders.

—Psalm 78:2–4 NLT

In The Parable of the Leaven, the Old Testament prophetic Scripture is fulfilled in the New Testament.

Fulfilling Scripture

All these things spake Jesus unto the multitude in parables; and without a parable spake he not unto them: That it might be fulfilled which was spoken by the prophet, saying, I will open my mouth in parables; I will utter things which have been kept secret from the foundation of the world.

—Matthew 13:34–35 KJV

Jesus spoke all these things to the crowd in parables; he did not say anything to them without using a parable. So was fulfilled what was spoken through the prophet: I will open my mouth in parables, I will utter things hidden since the creation of the world.

—Matthew 13:34–35 NIV

As a means of fulfilling the Old Testament scripture, Jesus uses parables no fewer than thirty-two times to extract His spiritual meaning from the natural examples provided. As we seek ways to strengthen our personal relationship with God, and to glory Him at all times, the parables of Jesus set forth a flawless road map, or guideline(s), to follow. Our spoken words, thoughts, and deeds (actions) should mirror the example that Jesus set for us all to follow. The following parables are worthy of examination:

Words (spoken)

Parable of the Soils

In this parable, Jesus is teaching a great multitude of people. Jesus' location is on a ship and the people are gathered on land nearby. As Jesus teaches, He urges His audience to listen intently to His message by uttering His famous quote, *"He that hath ears to hear, let him hear"* (Mark 4:9 KJV). Jesus' **words** are ministering life into those that have a desire to hear. Further, Jesus asks, *"Know ye not this parable? and how then will ye know all parables?"* (:13)

Jesus uses this parable to compare the sower of seeds (one who scatters seed on the ground, perhaps a farmer) and the sower that sows the Word (of God). For the farmer, not all seeds sown will mature and grow. Some will fall by the wayside and encounter the dangers of the stony ground, birds that eat them as food, the heat of the sun, and the thorns which choke the growth process. However, those that fall upon good ground, grow and mature to produce fruit. Likewise, for the sower of the Word, everyone that hears the Word of God will not grow and mature. For some, Satan will immediately come to take away the Word that was sown. For others, they will receive the Word gladly, but will not be equipped to endure hardship or persecution. Still for others, the cares (burdens) of everyday living and the deception of riches will make them unfruitful and unproductive. However, there will be those that will gladly hear the Word, receive it, and bear fruit, for the Word was sown on good ground.

Jesus admonishes us to speak uplifting and encouraging words to all of those within our sphere of influence. Not everyone that hears our message will respond alike. Those who have an ear to hear and act accordingly, will bear fruit and make a positive impact upon the lives that they influence each day.

And he began again to teach by the sea side: and there was gathered unto him a great multitude, so that he entered into a ship, and sat in the sea; and the whole multitude was by the sea on the land.

And he taught them many things by parables, and said unto them in his doctrine,
Hearken; Behold, there went out a sower to sow:

And in came to pass, as he sowed, some fell by the way side, and the fowls of the air came and devoured it up.

And some fell on stony ground, where it had not much earth; and immediately it sprang up, because it had no depth of earth:

But when the sun was up, it was scorched; and because it had no root, it withered away.

And some fell among thorns, and the thorns grew up, and choked it, and it yielded no fruit.

And other fell on good ground, and did yield fruit that sprang up and increased; and brought forth, some thirty, and some sixty, and some an hundred.

And he said unto them, He that hath ears to hear, let him hear.

And when he was alone, they that were about him with the twelve asked of him the parable.

And he said unto them, Unto you it is given to know the mystery of the kingdom of God: but unto them that are without, all these things are done in parables:

That SEEING THAT MAY SEE, AND NOT PERCEIVE; AND HEARING THEY MAY HEAR, AND NOT UNDERSTAND; LEST AT ANY TIME THEY SHOULD BE CONVERTED, AND THEIR SINS SHOULD BE FORGIVEN THEM.

And he said unto them, Know ye not this parable? and how then will ye know all parables?

The sower soweth the word.

And these are they by the way side, where the word is sown; but when they have heard, Satan cometh immediately, and taketh away the word that was sown in their hearts.

And these are they likewise which are sown on stony ground; who, when they have heard the word, immediately receive it with gladness;

And have no root in themselves, and so endure but for a time: afterward, when affliction or persecution ariseth for the word's sake, immediately they are offended.

And these are they which are sown among thorns; such as hear the word,

And the cares of this world, and the deceitfulness of riches, and the lusts of other things entering in, choke the word, and it becometh unfruitful.

And these are they which are sown on good ground; such as hear the word, and receive it, and bring forth fruit, some thirtyfold, some sixty, and some an hundred.

—Mark 4:1–20 KJV (emphasis added)

Once again Jesus began teaching by the lakeshore. A very large crowd soon gathered around him, so he got into a boat. Then he sat in the boat while all the people remained on the shore. He taught them by telling many stories in the form of parables, such as this one:

"Listen! A farmer went out to plant some seed.

As he scattered it across his field, some of the seed fell on a footpath, and the birds came and ate it.

Other seed fell on shallow soil with underlying rock. The seed sprouted quickly because the soil was shallow.

But the plant soon wilted under the hot sun, and since it didn't have deep roots, it died.

Other seed fell among thorns that grew up and choked out the tender plants so they produced no grain.

Still other seeds fell on fertile soil, and they sprouted, grew, and produced a crop that was thirty, sixty, and even a hundred times as much as had been planted!"

Then he said, "Anyone with ears to hear should listen and understand."

Later, when Jesus was alone with the twelve disciples and with the others who were gathered around, they asked him what the parables meant.

He replied, "You are permitted to understand the secret of the Kingdom of God. But I use parables for everything I say to outsiders, so that the Scriptures might be fulfilled: 'When they see what I do, they will learn nothing. When they hear what I say, they will not understand. Otherwise, they will turn to me and be forgiven.'"

Then Jesus said to them, "If you can't understand the meaning of this parable, how will you understand all the other parables?

The farmer plants seed by taking God's word to others.

The seed that fell on the footpath represents those who hear the message, only to have Satan come at once and take it away.

The seed on the rocky soil represents those who hear the message and immediately receive it with joy.

But since they don't have deep roots, they don't last long. They fall away as soon as they have problems or are persecuted for believing God's word.

The seed that fell among the thorns represents others who hear God's word,

but all too quickly the message is crowded out by the worries of this life, the lure of wealth, and the desire for other things, so no fruit is produced.

And the seed that fell on good soil represents those who hear and accept God's word and produce a harvest of thirty, sixty, or even a hundred times as much as had been planted!

—Mark 4:1–20 NLT

NOTES:

_____

_____

_____

_____

Thoughts

Parable of the Lost Sheep

In this parable, Jesus makes a profound statement concerning humility and His assignment in the earth. He is teaching His disciples about a ***thought process*** relative to all of God's people.

Our ***thought process*** should mirror Jesus' as we seek to glorify God in our lives.

In Matthew 18:3–5, Jesus has placed a little child in His midst, and before His disciples, to use as an object lesson. As a sign of humility, Jesus teaches us to become as humble as the child. He goes on to say that through the practice of humility, you and I are great in the kingdom of heaven. It is more important, based upon Jesus' teaching, to save one lost person (uses a sheep as the object lesson) who has gone astray than it is to care for the others (a herd of ninety-nine sheep) who are comfortable in their environment and are in no clear sign of danger. It is, therefore, better to rejoice in seeking and saving one from the crowd than it is to comfort the others who are able to maintain a safe haven on their own.

God does not want any of us to perish, nor others that we know (our sphere of influence), without first having an opportunity to "reconnect" with Him. This is a ***thought process*** that glorifies God. The relationship between humility and thought process(es) is patterned after Jesus' assignment in the earth *"to seek and to save that which was lost"* (Luke 19:10). As we fulfill our respective assignments on earth, and work dutifully within the body of Christ, we too will seek and save that one who has lost his way and is struggling in the wilderness.

For the Son of man is come to save that which was lost. How think ye? if a man have an hundred sheep, and one of them be gone astray, doth he not leave the ninety and nine, and goeth into the mountains, and seeketh that which is gone astray? And if so be that he find it, verily I say unto you, he rejoiceth more of that sheep, than of the ninety and nine which went not astray. Even so it is not the will of your Father which is in heaven, that one of these little ones should perish.

—Matthew 18:11–14 KJV

The Son of Man came to save lost people. If a man has a hundred sheep but one of the sheep gets lost, he will leave the other ninety-nine on the hill and go to look for the lost sheep. I tell you the truth, if he finds it he is happier about that one sheep than about the ninety-nine that were never lost. In the same way, your Father in heaven does not want any of these little children to be lost.

—Matthew 18:11–14 NCV

NOTES:

_____

_____

_____

_____

Deeds (actions)

Parable of the Mustard Seed

In this parable, Jesus uses the example of how the smallest seed known to man can, once planted, grows into the one of the largest plants in the world. Its branches are huge. So large that the birds can rest and lodge as they fly by.

In a similar fashion, our **deeds**, no matter how small, can bring forth a great return. A deed is simply defined as "something that is done." Our positive actions influence and touch the lives of others much more than we realize. It fosters a sense of security and love for the recipient. In turn, that identical deed or action is extended to others and so on and so on. Frequently, that action manifests its way into the lives of so many people that we may never know, but it was initially planted by one small positive deed (something that was done).

Again he said, "What shall we say the kingdom of God is like, or what parable shall we use to describe it? It is like a mustard seed, which is the smallest seed you plant in the ground. Yet when planted, it grows and becomes the largest of all garden plants, with such big branches that the birds of the air can perch in its shade."

—Mark 4:30–32 NIV

And he said, Whereunto shall we liken the kingdom of God? or with what comparison shall we compare it? It is like a grain of mustard seed, which, when it is sown in the earth, is less than all the seeds that be in the earth: But when it is sown, it groweth up, and becometh greater than all herbs, and shooteth out great branches; so that the fowls of the air may lodge under the shadow of it.

—Mark 4:30–32 KJV

God gives the increase to the seed that was planted. We sow, God works with it and causes it to grow and grow...

I planted, Apollos watered, but God [all the while] was making it grow and [He] gave the increase. So neither he who plants is anything nor he who waters, but [only] God Who makes it grow and become greater.

—1 Corinthians 3:6–7 Amplified

I have planted, A-pol'-los watered; but God gave the increase. So then neither is he that planteth any thing, neither he that watereth; but God that giveth the increase.

—1 Corinthians 3:6–7 KJV

So glorify God through words, thoughts, and deeds. That is what we are called to do.

And whatsoever ye do in word or deed, do all in the name of the Lord Jesus, giving thanks to God and the Father by him.

—Colossians 3:17 KJV

Everything you do or say should be done to obey Jesus your Lord. And in all you do, give thanks to God the Father through Jesus.

—Colossians 3:17 NCV

NOTES:

_____

_____

_____

_____

If a Christian is careless in Bible reading, he will care less about Christian living. It is therefore important to understand the parables of Jesus relative to how we glorify God.

OUR LIFESTYLE

Love the Lord your God with all your heart and with all your soul and with all your mind and with all your strength.

—Mark 12:30 NIV

AND THOU SHALL LOVE THE LORD THY GOD WITH ALL THY HEART, AND WITH ALL THY SOUL, AND WITH ALL THY MIND, AND WITH ALL THY STRENGTH: this is the first commandment.

—Mark 12:30 KJV (emphasis added)

Our Christlike conduct and character remain the strongest argument for our faith. Our lifestyle is a visible manifestation of our conduct and character. To *Give God the Glory!* there must be a *distinctively different lifestyle* that will cause others to inquire about (y)our source of peace, joy, love, and positive attributes. If you honor Christ in your heart, He will be honored by your life.

Howbeit Jesus suffered him not, but saith unto him, Go home to thy friends, and tell them how great things the Lord hath done for thee, and hath had compassion on thee.

—Mark 5:19 KJV

However, Jesus did not permit him, but said to him, "Go home to your friends, and tell them what great things the Lord has done for you, and how He has had compassion on you."

—Mark 5:19 NKJV

Distinctively Different

Jesus called His followers to be "salt and light." As *salt*, we are to act as a preservative, penetrating the culture to help sustain what is good and right. As *light*, we are to counter the darkness and bring forth truth and righteousness. Jesus said that we are salt and light, but He warned against losing our saltiness and hiding our light (Matthew 5:13–20). Here are two safeguards to prevent this from happening:

- ✓ Salt as a seasoning is useless unless it is in contact with food and mixed into it. Jesus calls us to "flavor" society in His name through close involvement with people.
- ✓ Light is meant to be visible. Secret believers need to come out of hiding and be known as disciples. Their profession of faith must become self-evident through their good works.[2]

You are the salt of the earth. But if the salt loses its salty taste, it cannot be made salty again. It is good for nothing, except to be thrown out and walked on. You are the light that gives light to the world. A city that is built on a hill cannot be hidden. And people don't hide a light under a bowl. They put it on a lampstand so the light shines for all the people in the house. In the same way, you should be a light for other people. Live so that they will see the good things you do and will praise your Father in heaven.

—Matthew 5:13–16 NCV

Ye are the salt of the earth: but if the salt have lost his savour, wherewith shall it be salted? it is thenceforth good for nothing, but to be cast out, and to be trodden under foot of men. Ye are the light of the world. A city that is set on an hill cannot be hid. Neither do men light a candle, and put it under a bushel, but on a candlestick; and it giveth light unto all that are in the house. Let your light so shine before men, that they may see your good works, and glorify your Father which is in heaven.

—Matthew 5:13–16 KJV

Salt

Salt is used to preserve, season, cure, or save for future use. It changes everything that it touches! Hence, a salty Christian makes others thirsty for Jesus, who is the water of life. Salt can be thought of as a fertilizer to promote growth and development, it is used to purify, and it is used to correct or improve conditions in its surroundings.

NOTES:

_____

_____

_____

_____

Light

Light is defined as something that makes things visible or affords illumination. Without the light of God's spirit, we will be in the dark about God's Word. The scriptures characterize light in many different forms, for example:

In the beginning God created the heavens and the earth. Now the earth was formless and empty, darkness was over the surface of the deep, and the Spirit of God was hovering over the waters. And God said, "Let there be light," and there was light. God saw that the light was good, and He separated the light from the darkness.

—Genesis 1:1–4 NIV

In the beginning God created the heaven and the earth. And the earth was without form, and void; and darkness was upon the face of the deep. And the Spirit of God moved upon the face of the waters. And God said, Let there be light: and there was light. And God saw the light, that it was good: and God divided the light from the darkness.

—Genesis 1:1–4 KJV

Once more Jesus addressed the crowd. He said, I am the Light of the world. He who follows Me will not be walking in the dark, but will have the Light which is Life.

—John 8:12 Amplified

Then spake Jesus again unto them, saying, I am the light of the world: he that followeth me shall not walk in darkness, but shall have the light of life.

—John 8:12 KJV

And this is the condemnation, that light is come into the world, and men loved darkness rather than light, because their deeds were evil. For every one that doeth evil hateth the light, neither cometh to the light, lest his deeds should be reproved. But he that doeth truth cometh to the light, that his deeds may be made manifest, that they are wrought in God.

—John 3:19–21 KJV

The Light has come into the world. And the light is the test by which men are guilty or not. People love darkness more than the light because the things they do are sinful. Everyone who sins hates the Light. He stays away from the Light because his sin would be found out. The man who does what is right comes to the Light. What he does will be seen because he has done what God wanted him to do.

—John 3:19–21 NLV

NOTES:

_____

_____

_____

_____

The Colors of Light

White—the white light contains all colors.

Red—the color of intense, physical energy. When you need a powerful burst of energy, imagine red or look at something red.

Orange—the next color in the spectrum. It is a color of energy, too, but a quieter, more sustaining energy; a more enduring strength.

Yellow—the color of the mind—joyful, purifying, mental energy. It is the color of lemons, smiley faces (buttons), and dishwashing detergent. Yellow light brings clarity. The thing we most often associate with yellow is the sun.

Green—the color of healing and the color of learning; brilliant, emerald green (See Psalm 23—Appendix B). Healing and learning are active processes. When you think of green, think of actively healing yourself, through physical action and through active visualizations. Think of vigorously learning all you can about yourself and your life.

Blue—a color of spirit, calm, and peace. As the sun is yellow and usually associated with sunny thoughts, so the sky is high and blue, and the sea is deep and blue.

Purple—the color of royalty—the inner royalty that is the true you and the outer royalty of the Divine. Use purple when you want to feel cloaked in the grand, magnificent, noble, majestic, and stately presence within you.

NOTES:

_____

_____

_____

_____

THE HUMAN BODY

The key to understanding life is in the source of life, not in life itself. We are one of a kind; designed to glorify God as only you and I can.

Thank you for making me so wonderfully complex! Your workmanship is marvelous— how well I know it. You watched me as I was being formed in utter seclusion, as I was woven together in the dark of the womb.

—Psalm 139:14–15 NLT

I will praise thee; for I am fearfully and wonderfully made: marvellous of thy works; and that my soul knoweth right well. My substance was not hid from thee, when I was made in secret, and curiously wrought in the lowest parts of the earth.

—Psalm 139:14–15 KJV

What? Know ye not that your body is the temple of the Holy Ghost which is in you, which ye have of God, and ye are not your own?

—1 Corinthians 6:19 KJV

Do you not know that your body is a temple of the Holy Spirit, who is in you, whom you have received from God? You are not your own.

—1 Corinthians 6:19 NIV

For in him we live, and move, and have our being; as certain also of your own poets have said, For we are also his offspring.

—Acts 17:28 KJV

But even the very hairs of your head are all numbered. Fear not therefore: ye are of more value than many sparrows.

—Luke 12:7 KJV

Our human body was specifically designed to relate to the physical realm. The triune nature of man is designed for the following purposes:

Table 1. Triune Nature of Man

Man's spirit	To relate to God (spirit world)
Man's soul	To relate to the mental realm (intelligence)
Man's body	**To relate to the physical environment (earth)**

Our human bodies are awesome! It's one prime biological function—to reproduce itself and ensure the survival of its offspring. The ten major systems of the body are:

✓ Skeletal
✓ Muscular
✓ Cardiovascular
✓ Nervous
✓ Endocrine
✓ Immune
✓ Digestive
✓ Reproductive
✓ Urinary
✓ Respiratory

Cells

Our cells are the fundamental units of life. They are the smallest structure of the body capable of performing all the processes that define life, including respiration, movement, digestion, and reproduction, although not every cell can perform all of these functions. Most are invisible to the naked eye.

The Skeleton System

On average, there are 206 bones of varying shapes and sizes. Bone is a type of connective tissue that is as strong as steel but as light as aluminum. It is made up of specialized cells and protein fibers interwoven in a gel-like matrix composed of water, mineral salts, and carbohydrates. The rib cage alone has 12 pairs of ribs that attach to the spine. Another 22 bones surround the cranial cavity protecting the brain and face.

There is more life in a bone than most people think. The living skeleton, although tough, is a flexible structure with blood flowing through every part, and it is in a state of constant growth and remodeling. Even bones discovered by archaeologists tell a story—they often reveal a great deal about the dead person's age, sex, height and weight, activities, and whether he or she was a meat-eater or vegetarian. Living bones are actually a moist hive of activity. The marrow in bones is the site where red blood cells and some types of white blood cells are produced.

The Muscular System

Muscles make up the bulk of the body and account for about half its weight. Over 600 skeletal muscles are present in our bodies.

The Nervous System

Our brains—not our hearts—are where we feel emotions such as love and anger. They are also where we think, decide, and initiate and control our actions. Communications between the billions of nerve cells in the brain is by means of chemical signals as well as electrical ones, which is why alcohol and drugs affect us. The brain is capable of creativity in a way no computer has yet achieved. But it is delicate, for if nerve tracts within the brain or spinal cord are damaged by injury or disease, they are unable to repair themselves.

The body and brain are constantly alive with billions of electrical and chemical signals. The basic unit of the nervous system is the neuron. The body of this specialized nerve cell has projections that either receive electrical messages from or transmit messages to other neurons, muscles, or glands. The billions of interconnecting neurons that make up the nervous system are protected by other supporting nerve cells known as glial cells.

Our brain

The brain is composed of more than 12 billion neurons and 50 billion supporting glial cells, but it weighs less than 3 pounds.

IBM has built a new supercomputer capable of 12 *trillion* calculations per second (12.3 teraflops). ASCI White, an RS/6000 SP supercomputer, is physically as large as two basketball courts, and will be used to test the safety and reliability of the United States' nuclear weapons stockpile without real-world testing. The system is powered by 8,192 copper microprocessors, contains more than 6 terabytes of memory and more than 160 terabytes of disk storage capability.[3] Even with this latest invention, it still cannot compare to the functionality of the human brain.

Our spinal cord

The spinal cord is a cable about 17 inches in length that descends from the brain to the lumbar part of the back. Through 31 pairs of spinal nerves, the spinal cord is connected to the rest of the body and relays information received by way of these nerves about its internal and external environment to and from the brain.

The Cardiovascular System
The heart and circulation
Blood is pumped out from the heart through strong, elastic tubes called arteries. Vessels leaving the right ventricle initiate the pulmonary circulatory system, which carries deoxygenated blood to the lungs for replenishment with fresh oxygen. The aorta, the single main artery from the left ventricle, branches to form the systemic circulation, which takes oxygen to all body tissues. Another network of veins returns deoxygenated blood to the heart. The smallest arteries (arterioles) and veins (venules) are linked by tiny capillaries. This system is 90,000 miles long! On average, blood completes a full circuit of the body in approximately one minute! The full circuit around the lungs and body takes only approximately one minute when the body is at rest, and the heart pumps about 5 to 7 quarts of blood a day. The heart forces blood around an impressive network of blood vessel that would circle the Earth two and one-half times.

Studies and research on blood type reveal four primary categories for all human kind. The blood type and percentage of each type is as follows:

Blood Type	Percent of human population
O Positive	37.4%
A Positive	35.7%
A Negative	6.3%
B Negative	1.5%

The rarest, AB Negative, is found in only 1 in 167 people, or 0.6% of the population.

The Immune System
The body has its very own security force—the immune system—that patrols the body and guards it against invasion from outside and subversion from within.

The Respiratory System
Our lungs are second only to the heart in their work rate. Each lung expands and contracts between 12 and 20 times a minute to supply the body with the oxygen it needs and to expel carbon dioxide.

At a keynote address, during a prayer breakfast, entitled "Building Winners—On and Off the Field," Head Football Coach Lou Holtz used the podium to tell his audience on just how awesome the human body is. He boldly articulated many of the fine details of the human body and its unique composition. His keynote was delivered sometime after the Division I college football national championship game between the University of Notre Dame and the University of Southern California, in which Notre Dame came from behind to win in January 1989. Coach Holtz enthusiastically educates the audience and goes on to say,

We are important. We are not blind because we have 100 million receptors that can see. We are not deaf because we have 24 thousand fibers that can hear. Your brain weighs 3 pounds and you have 13 billion nerve cells—double the number of people on Earth. You have over 500 muscles, over 200 bones, and 7 miles of nerve fibers. There are 36 billion beats of the heart per year and your skin will not rust as it replaces itself daily. There are 200 trillion blood cells in each quart of blood and 1 million molecules in each blood cell. Within each cell, there is an oscillator and each day, 200 million blood cells die and are replaced. You have 4 million pairs of sensitive structures. Man could not create a machine such as this. You are not going to tell me that this happened by accident.

While man makes continued attempts to figure out the human body, and all of its complexities, God is to be glorified for the marvelous work that He created. Below are two articles and reports that reference the millions of tax dollars that are spent to try to understand just how awesome we are:

1. The front page article entitled, "Genetic Code of Human Life is Cracked by Scientists,"[4] (*The New York Times*, June 27, 2000), provides a comprehensive report on the conclusions of the first survey of the human genome, as offered by Francis S. Collins, head of the Human Genome Project, and J. Craig Venter, head of Celera Genomics.

2. Further, U.S. News and World Report featured an article entitled, "We've only just begun: Gene map in hand, the hunt for proteins is on."[5] The writer of the article, Joannie Schrof Fischer, says that

The researchers have announced that they have successfully mapped the human genome, the famous DNA strand of more than 3 million chemical 'letters' that spell out instructions for how to build a human being. Yet, despite the grand aura of the double helix, knowing its code is really only a means to a greater end. To learn what makes the human body thrive or falter, scientists will now brave an endeavor that dwarfs the genome project. Welcome to the age of 'proteomics,' jargon for the study of proteins, the most complex of all known molecules. All in all, the body may have 2 million or more distinct proteins. And a single protein is so complex that IBM plans to spend the next five years deciphering how just one particular protein forms its unique shape. To do that, the company will need to create a computer 500 times as powerful as any in existence today and 40 times as fast as today's 40 fastest machines working in concert.

Where does it stop? Man continues to try to figure out what only God can create and fully understand.

NOTES:

_____

_____

_____

_____

OUR FAITH

Faith is a law.

Where, then, is boasting? It is excluded. On what principle? On that of observing the law? No, but on that of faith. For we maintain that a man is justified by faith apart from observing the law.

—Romans 3:27–28 NIV

Where is boasting then? It is excluded. By what law? of works? Nay: but by the law of faith. Therefore we conclude that a man is justified by faith without the deeds of the law.

—Romans 3:27–28 KJV

Faith applies to everyone.

Therefore being justified by faith, we have peace with God through our Lord Jesus Christ: By whom also we have access by faith into this grace wherein we stand, and rejoice in hope of the glory of God.

—Romans 5:1–2 KJV

Faith comes by hearing...and hearing...and hearing.

So then faith cometh by hearing, and hearing by the word of God.

—Romans 10:17 KJV

Without it, it is impossible to please God.

But without faith it is impossible to please him: for he that cometh to God must believe that he is, and that he is a rewarder of them that diligently seek him.

—Hebrews 11:6 KJV

Fight the good fight of faith, lay hold on eternal life, whereunto thou art also called, and hast professed a good profession before many witnesses.

—1 Timothy 6:12 KJV

Only faith pleases God and it is through faith that believers procure things in the spirit realm. In the natural realm, we rely on currency to buy things; the concept is the same. Simply put, faith is the character trait that distinguishes the believer (saint) from the rest of the world.

Now faith is the substance of things hoped for, the evidence of things not seen.

—Hebrews 11:1 KJV

It is by faith that we believe, although we do not quite understand, that the worlds were framed by God. It is by faith that we believe that man was created by God and was given life when God breathed the breath of life through Adam's nostrils (Genesis 2:7). Therefore, faith is manifested in our hope that things unseen are indeed reality. This hope is heightened as we glorify God at all times. Acting upon our faith causes positive results in our lives.

> *For as the body without the spirit is dead, so faith without works is dead also.*
>
> —James 2:26 KJV

It is by faith that we know that God is the creator of:

...all things

> *Thou art worthy, O Lord, to receive glory and honour and power: for thou hast created all things, and for thy pleasure they are and were created.*
>
> —Revelation 4:11 KJV

> *For by him were all things created, that are in heaven, and that are in earth, visible and invisible, whether they be thrones, or dominions, or principalities, or powers: all things were created by him, and for him:*
>
> —Colossians 1:16 KJV

...heaven and earth

> *Our help is in the name of the LORD, who made heaven and earth.*
>
> —Psalm 124:8 KJV

> *My help cometh from the LORD, which made heaven and earth.*
>
> —Psalm 121:2 KJV

> *And, Thou, Lord, in the beginning hast laid the foundation of the earth; and the heavens are the works of thine hands:*
>
> —Hebrews 1:10 KJV

> *Of old hast thou laid the foundation of the earth: and the heavens are the work of thy hands.*
>
> —Psalm 102:25 KJV

> *For all the gods of the nations are idols: but the LORD made the heavens.*
>
> —Psalm 96:5 KJV

Thou, even thou, art LORD alone; thou hast made heaven, the heaven of heavens, with all their host, the earth, and all things that are therein, the seas, and all that is therein, and thou preservest them all; and the host of heaven worshippeth thee.

—Nehemiah 9:6 KJV

Then the channels of waters were seen, and the foundations of the world were discovered at thy rebuke, O LORD, at the blast of the breath of thy nostrils.

—Psalm 18:15 KJV

The earth is the LORD's, and the fulness thereof; the world, and they that dwell therein. For he hath founded it upon the seas, and established it upon the floods.

—Psalm 24:1–2 KJV

Before the mountains were brought forth, or ever thou hadst formed the earth and the world, even from everlasting to everlasting, thou art God.

—Psalm 90:2 KJV

...the beginning

In the beginning God created the heaven and the earth.

—Genesis 1:1 KJV

In the beginning was the Word, and the Word was with God, and the Word was God. The same was in the beginning with God. All things were made by him; and without him was not any thing made that was made.

—John 1:1–3 KJV

...the foundations of the earth

Who laid the foundations of the earth, that it should not be removed for ever.

—Psalm 104:5 KJV

NOTES:

_____

_____

_____

_____

...the sun, moon, stars, and heaven

Praise ye the LORD. Praise ye the LORD from the heavens: praise him in the heights. Praise ye him, all his angels: praise ye him, all his hosts. Praise ye him, sun and moon: praise him, all ye stars of light. Praise him, ye heavens of heavens, and ye waters that be above the heavens. Let them praise the name of the LORD: for he commanded, and they were created.

—Psalm 148:1–5 KJV

...the ends of the earth

Hath thou not known? hast thou not heard, that the everlasting God, the LORD, the Creator of the ends of the earth, fainteth not, neither is weary? there is no searching of his understanding.

—Isaiah 40:28 KJV

...lightning, rain, and wind

When he uttereth his voice, there is a multitude of waters in the heavens, and he causeth the vapours to ascend from the ends of the earth; he maketh lightnings with rain, and bringeth forth the wind out of his treasures.

—Jeremiah 10:13 KJV

He causeth the vapours to ascend from the ends of the earth; he maketh lightnings for the rain; he bringeth the wind out of his treasuries.

—Psalm 135:7 KJV

When he uttereth his voice, there is a multitude of waters in the heavens; and he causeth the vapors to ascend from the ends of the earth: he maketh lightnings with rain, and bringeth forth the wind out of his treasures.

—Jeremiah 51:16 KJV

Hear attentively the noise of his voice, and the sound that goeth out of his mouth. He directeth it under the whole heaven, and his lightning unto the ends of the earth. After it a voice roareth: he thundereth with the voice of his excellency; and he will not stay them when his voice is heard. God thundereth marvellously with his voice; great things doeth he, which we cannot comprehend. For he saith to the snow, Be thou on the earth; likewise to the small rain, and to the great rain of his strength.

—Job 37:2–6 KJV

...the seasons

And I will make them and the places round about my hill be a blessing; and I will cause the shower to come down in his season; there shall be showers of blessing.

—Ezekiel 34:26 KJV

By the breath of God frost is given: and the breadth of the waters is straitened.

—Job 37:10 KJV

Daniel answered and said, Blessed be the name of God for ever and ever: for wisdom and might are his: And he changeth the times and the seasons: he removeth kings, and setteth up kings: he giveth wisdom unto the wise, and knowledge to them that know understanding:

—Daniel 2:20–21 KJV

...all people

And God said, Let us make man in our image, after our likeness...So God created man in his own image, in the image of God created he him; male and female created he them.

—Genesis 1:26–27 KJV

Have we not all one father? hath not one God created us? why do we deal treacherously every man against his brother, by profaning the covenant of our fathers?

—Malachi 2:10 KJV

...other worlds

Through faith we understand that the worlds were framed by the word of God, so that things which are seen were not made of things which do appear.

—Hebrews 11:3 KJV

God, who at sundry times and in divers manners spake in time past unto the fathers by the prophets, Hath in these last days spoken unto us by his Son, whom he hath appointed heir of all things, by whom also he made the worlds;

—Hebrews 1:1–2 KJV

NOTES:

_____

_____

_____

_____

Man tries, but only God knows. Attempts to apply human logic to God's sovereignty (God does not need permission to do the things that He does) remain unfruitful. While scientists are still attempting to devise new ways to collect and analyze unearthly signals, the signs of intelligent life remain undetectable. In *The New York Times* article entitled, "Astronomers Revive Scan of the Heavens for Signs of Life," by William J. Broad (September 29, 1998), it is reported that astronomers are concentrating intensely on proving that the Milky Way is approximately 100,000 light-years in diameter. Over the next few years, astronomers at the SETI Institute plan to use the massive Arecibo radiotelescope to listen for signals from alien civilizations. Their search will encompass some 1,000 of the galaxy's 400 billion stars, all within the relatively close distance of 200 light-years.

Further, the Hubble Space Telescope, named after astronomer Edwin Hubble, has been in orbit since April 1990. The telescope is revolutionizing what astronomers know about the cosmos. Making 5,800 orbits each year, Hubble is able to see distant objects 10 times more clearly than the best observatories on the ground. In the *USA Today* article entitled, "Hubble Telescope: A Decade in Space, Hubble's 10 Great Discoveries" (November 5, 1999), some of the key discoveries include:

✓ The approximate age of the universe is 12 to 14 billion years;
✓ Quasars can be clearly seen at the center of galaxies and are thought to act as the power plants that cause galaxies to merge with each other and form new quasars;
✓ Galaxies 12 billion light-years away are clearly seen; and
✓ Exploding stars, called supernovae, can be distinguished from the rest of their galaxies. Astronomers now know how stars change over time and use the data to calculate distances in the universe.

Other efforts to find "evidence" of biblical truths persist. Non-believers continue to question God's sovereignty. Published articles continue to flood the newsstands in a desperate search to "prove" what has been revealed in *The Holy Bible*. In the five articles referenced below, the titles speak for themselves relative to doubt and lack of faith:

✓ "For Noah's Flood, a New Wave of Evidence," Guy Guglioatta, *The Washington Post*, November 18, 1999.

This article focuses on the discovery, by scientists, of an ancient coastline 550 feet below the surface of the Black Sea. This, in their mind(s), provides dramatic new evidence of a sudden, catastrophic flood around 7,500 years ago; the possible source of the Old Testament story of Noah.

✓ "An enduring mystery (evidence points to a flood of biblical proportions)," Michael Satchell, *U.S. News and World Report*, September 25, 2000.

This article provides more insight into how, in 1949, a U.S. spy plane flew over mountains in northern Turkey and photographed what appeared to be the outline of an ancient vessel (that is, Noah's Ark) on the side of a glacier. The site of Mount Ararat, as named in Genesis, is the place where the ark came to rest. The Central Intelligence Agency, once becoming involved, kept it under wraps for 40 years.

✓ Hell Hath No Fury (with fire and brimstone out of fashion, modern thinking says the netherworld isn't so hot afterall)," Jeffery L. Sheler, *U.S. News and World Report*, January 31, 2000, p. 45.

The following two tables present an overview of this article based upon the results of two separate surveys:

Table 2. Survey of Existence of Hell

DO YOU THINK THERE IS A HELL?	PERCENTAGE OF RESPONSES
Yes	64%
No	25%
Don't Know	9%

Table 3. Ideas of Hell

WHAT COMES CLOSEST TO YOUR IDEA OF HELL?	1997	NOW
Hell is a real place where people suffer eternal fiery torments	48%	34%
Hell is an anguished state of existence eternally separated from god	46%	53%
Don't know	4%	11%

✓ "Is the Bible True?" by Jeffery L. Sheler, *U.S. News and World Report*, October 25, 1999, p. 50.

This article centers around biblical topics such as "in the beginning," "the age of the patriarchs," the "flight from Egypt," the "rule of David," the "days of Jesus," and "the road ahead."

✓ "Why Did He Die? Jesus put the kingdom of God up against Caesar. And that act led to a political execution that launched a major world religion," Jeffery L. Sheler, *U.S. News and World Report*, April 24, 2000, p. 50.

This article prepares the reader for the annual Holy Week observances (Easter) by attempting to explain Jesus' death and crucifixion.

By faith, we can understand and appreciate God for who He is. He is omnipresent (present everywhere), omniscient (having complete or unlimited knowledge and awareness), and omnipotent (infinite in power; unlimited authority). We see His creation all around us. Man will only come to know and understand all of God's creation *in part* because only God is all-knowing. Do not allow the measure of faith that has been extended to you waver nor falter. While man continues to seek after physical evidence to prove what God has created, the truth has already been revealed in the hearts and minds of those who believe by faith—through His Word.

STUDY QUESTIONS AND DISCUSSION

Chapter One

1.   Does your life glorify God? (Matthew 6:24 and Colossians 3:17)

_____

_____

_____

       In word *(what you say)*? _____

       In thought *(what you think)*? _____

       In deeds *(your actions)*? _____

2.   Are you still seeking "physical evidence" that the Word of God is true?

_____

_____

_____

3.   What will you do today to take better care of your body which God has entrusted unto you? (1 Corinthians 3:16 and 6:19)

_____

_____

_____

4.   Do you walk by faith or walk by sight? (Romans 5:7; 2 Corinthians 5:7; Hebrews 10:23 and 38; Habakkuk 2:4; and Mark 11:22)

_____

_____

_____

5.   What places do you frequent where your "light" can/should shine brighter to glorify God for the things that He has done?

_____

_____

_____

Chapter Two

You're Called (whether you know it or not)

We are born with a Godly purpose to fulfill in this earth. Our Godly purpose cannot become a reality until we are first *reconnected* with the creator (God), through Jesus Christ. This first step, salvation, paves the way toward the recognition and acknowledgment of our assignment in the earth—*To seek and to save those who were lost (Luke 19:10 and Matthew 18:11).* How we each fulfill that respective assignment differently, yet the objective is the same: Love God, hate sin, and spread the gospel (good news!).

Then the word of the Lord came unto me, saying, Before I formed thee in the belly I knew thee; and before thou camest forth out of the womb I sanctified thee, and I ordained thee a prophet unto the nations.

—Jeremiah 1:4–5 KJV

But ye are a chosen generation, a royal priesthood, an holy nation, a peculiar people; that ye should shew forth the praises of him who hath called you out of darkness into his marvellous light: Which in time past were not a people, but are now the people of God: which had not obtained mercy, but now have obtained mercy.

—1 Peter 2:9–10 KJV

*T*o know God is to glorify Him through recognition and acknowledgment of our "calling." We are ALL called to do something. Not necessarily on a large scale, but to be productive and content within the vocation in which we are called. Unfulfillment is a sign of not operating within our calling. A key to acknowledging our calling begins with reconnecting to God. For we were created by Him, thus, to have life means that we must be connected to Him.

Our assignment in the earth is to seek and to save those who were lost (Luke 19:10 and Matthew 18:11). How we carry out our assignment is directly linked to our calling and our ability to recognize and acknowledge it. Sensitivity to our work within the Kingdom of God will significantly alter, for the positive, our management of time as well. God granted us all the same 24 hours in each day, so our calling will help us to focus more time on work for the Lord in lieu of worldly "things."

In this chapter, God encourages each of us to value the power of our preordained purpose *(calling)* for being birthed into the earth. He admonishes us to accept the free gift of salvation, to change our attitude, and to develop a deeper appreciation of time. God demonstrates in four ways how He is glorified through our calling. They are through:

✓ Our predetermined ordination—an examination of Jeremiah 1:4–5;
✓ Salvation—the new birth;
✓ Our attitude toward our *calling*—the key mental attribute toward success with God; and
✓ Time values—how we manage time.

<u>Central Theme</u>: Recognize and acknowledge your calling.
<u>Keyword</u>: Calling

Calling defined:

Qārā (Old Testament) is a verb and means "to call, call out, recite," "to call out loudly," "to summon," "to proclaim," or "to announce." This root word occurs in Old Aramaic, Canaanite, and Ugaritic, and other Semitic languages (except Ethiopic). The word appears in all periods of biblical Hebrew.

Naming a thing is frequently an assertion of sovereignty over it, which is the case in the first use of qara: "And God called the light Day, and the darkness he called Night" (Genesis 1:5). God's act of creating (naming) and numbering includes the stars (Psalm 147:4) and all other things (Isaiah 40:26). He allowed Adam to "name" the animals as a concrete demonstration of man's relative sovereignty over them (Genesis 2:19).

This verb also is used to indicate "calling to a specific task." Israel was called (elected) by God to be His people (Isaiah 65:12), as were the Gentiles in the messianic age (Isaiah 55:5).

Klēsis (New Testament) is a noun. "A calling" is always used in the New Testament of that calling the origin, nature, and destiny of which are heavenly (the idea of invitation being implied). It is used especially of God's invitation to man to accept the benefits of salvation (Romans 11:29 and 1 Corinthians 1:26 and 7:20) said there of the condition in which the calling finds one.

A PREDETERMINED ORDINATION

Knowing who we are, and what our purpose is, requires obedience to the law—both of man and God. Natural and spiritual laws are built-in and inseparable from our everyday existence. God demands that we obey the natural laws of the land, which can be seen, in order to have an appreciation for spiritual laws, which cannot be seen. As we strive to master our predetermined calling, lawful obedience is key to our success.

Acting contrary to our created role is death. Nothing can exist outside of this created role. We are made to be citizens of the kingdom of God (Romans 8:14–16 and Matthew 16:18).

NOTES:

_____

_____

_____

_____

We were made to fellowship with God, to have a relationship with God, and represent God on this earth.

Jeremiah the prophet

The book of Jeremiah, written by Jeremiah, is the prophecy of a man divinely called in his youth (about 20 years old) from the priest-city of Anathoth (a city two miles north of Jerusalem). Jeremiah is a heartbroken prophet (also referred to as the "weeping" prophet) with similar message, who labors for more than 40 years proclaiming a message of doom to the "stuck-in-their-ways" people of Judah. Through his sermons and signs he faithfully declares that surrender to God's will is the *only way to escape calamity*. References to him as the "weeping" prophet stem beyond the fact that he also wrote the book of Lamentations, which describes the funeral of a city. He was all along a mournful spectator of the sins of his people and of the desolated judgments that were coming upon them.

The book of Jeremiah is a record of the ministry of one of Judah's greatest prophets during its darkest days. He was not allowed to marry, was threatened in his hometown, tried for his life by the priests and prophets of Jerusalem, put in stocks, forced to flee from king Jehoiakim, publicly humiliated by the false prophet Hananiah, and thrown into cistern (a reservoir or tank for storing water). Despite the persecution, he faithfully proclaims the divine condemnation of rebellious Judah for 40 years and is rewarded with opposition, beatings, isolations, and imprisonment. Hence, his sympathy and sensitivity cause him to grieve over the rebelliousness and imminent doom of his nation. Judgment cannot be halted!

Ultimately, Jeremiah's 40-year declaration of doom is vindicated in an event so significant that it is recorded in detail four times in the scriptures as *The Fall of Jerusalem:*

- ✓ Jeremiah 39
- ✓ Jeremiah 52
- ✓ 2 Kings 25:2
- ✓ 2 Chronicles 36:13–21

Our calling

The LORD *spoke his word to me, saying: "Before I made you in your mother's womb, I chose you. Before you were born, I set you apart for a special work. I appointed you as a prophet to the nations.*

—Jeremiah 1:4–5 NCV

Then the word of the Lord came unto me, saying, Before I formed thee in the belly I knew thee; and before thou cameth forth out of the womb I sanctified thee, and I ordained thee a prophet unto the nations.

—Jeremiah 1:4–5 KJV

Jeremiah 1:4–5 is one of the most significant scriptures in the Old Testament. It is a very clear revelation that each of us were birthed into the earth for a *purpose*. We were called by an omnipotent God, creator of all things, to do something special. Even before our great grandparents knew one another, according to this scripture, God had established an intimate relationship with us. We were sanctified and ordained—to do something! Four key words stand out in this scripture:

"I knew thee"
- ✓ Knew—"intimately acquainted with." There are three versions of the original Hebrew words: *proginosko, epiginosko,* and *ginosko*. Each are more representative of "know" (present tense) than "knew" (past tense).

    proginosko means to know the truth before hand;

    epiginosko means to have a perception of the truth. To be very detailed and knowledgable to a particular subject; and *ginosko* means to come to know, understand, and accept fully while walking in progressional knowledge.

NOTES:

_____

_____

_____

_____

"I sanctified thee"
- ✓ Sanctified—"holy ones" and is derived from the Greek word *hagioi*. It is not an attainment, but the state into which God, by grace, calls sinful men, and in which they begin their course as Christians.

NOTES:

_____

_____

_____

_____

"I ordained thee"
- ✓ Ordained—"to divide, separate, decide, judge" and is derived from the Greek word *krinō*.

NOTES:

_____

_____

_____

_____

"a prophet unto the nations"
- ✓ Prophet—"one who speaks forth or openly; a proclaimer of a divine message" and is derived from the Greek word *prophētōs*. Biblical examples include Ezekiel, Jeremiah, and Isaiah.

God is intimately acquainted with His creation. We are declared holy ones who are separated from the system of this world to proclaim a divine message. That divine message is to proclaim that Jesus is Lord and to seek and to save those who were lost. We are ambassadors for Christ in the earth realm. We are called to reconcile those within our sphere of influence to Christ—the ministry of reconciliation. That is *our* job (assignment). Yes, each of us are blessed with different gifts, skills, and abilities, but ultimately the assignment is the same—to win souls for Christ. (Emphasis is added in the following scriptures.)

*And all things are of God, who hath reconciled us to himself by Jesus Christ, and hath given to us the **ministry of reconciliation**;*

—2 Corinthians 5:18 KJV

*And all of this is a gift from God, who brought us back to himself through Christ. And God has given us this task of **reconciling people to him**.*

—2 Corinthians 5:18 NLT

*Wherefore also we pray always for you, that our God would count you **worthy of this calling**, and fulfil all the good pleasure of his goodness, and the work of faith with power: That the name of our Lord Jesus Christ may be glorified in you, and ye in him, according to the grace of our God and the Lord Jesus Christ.*

—2 Thessalonians 1:11–12 KJV

*With this in mind, we constantly pray for you, that our God may count you **worthy of his calling**, and that by his power he may fulfill every good purpose of yours and every act prompted by your faith. We pray this so that the name of our Lord Jesus may be glorified in you, and you in him, according to the grace of our God and the Lord Jesus Christ.*

—2 Thessalonians 1:11–12 NIV

My brothers and sisters, try hard to be certain that you really are called and chosen by God. If you do all these things, you will never fall.

—1 Peter 1:10 NCV

*Wherefore the rather, brethen, give diligence to make your calling and election **sure**: for if ye do these things, ye shall never fall:*

—2 Peter 1:10 KJV

NOTES:

_____

_____

_____

_____

*Who has saved us and **called us to a holy life**—not because of anything we have done but because of his own purpose and grace. This grace was given us in Christ Jesus before the beginning of time.*

—2 Timothy 1:9 NIV

*Who hath saved us, and **called us with an holy calling**, not according to our works, but according to his own purpose and grace, which was given us in Christ Jesus before the world began,*

—2 Timothy 1:9 KJV

*And God said, **Let us make man in our image, after our likeness**: and let them have dominion over the fish of the sea, over the fowl of the air, and over the cattle, and over all the earth, and over every creeping thing that creepeth upon the earth.*

—Genesis 1:26 KJV

*God said, "Let Us [Father, Son, and Holy Spirit] make mankind in **Our image, after Our likeness**, and let them have complete authority over the fish of the sea, the birds of the air, the [tame] beasts, and over all of the earth, and over everything that creeps upon the earth."*

—Genesis 1:26 Amplified

*The heaven, even the heavens, are the LORD's: but **the earth hath he given to the children of men**.*

—Psalm 115:16 KJV

*Heaven belongs to the Lord, but **he gave the earth to people**.*

—Psalm 115:16 NCV

NOTES:

_____

_____

_____

_____

Samuel's Story[6]

The story of little Samuel is an excellent example of our calling. Samuel, a 21-week-old pre-born baby (fetus), was being operated on by a surgeon named Joseph Bruner (Vanderbilt University Medical Center in Nashville, TN). A 21-week-old fetus can be legally aborted in the U.S. The baby had been diagnosed with spina bifida, which leaves the spinal cord (backbone) exposed after it fails to develop properly. The corrective surgery was performed inside of the mother's womb despite the fact that it had never been performed on a fetus this young and the procedure had not yet been endorsed in medical journals. To operate on such a tiny baby would require special miniature instruments to be created. The sutures used, for example, were less than the thickness of a human hair. A Caesarean section was then performed to lift the uterus gently from the mother's body, permitting the surgeon to make a small incision through which the operation would be performed.

It was at this precise time that the baby's fully-developing hand wrapped itself around the finger of the surgeon. The photograph captures that amazing moment with perfect clarity.

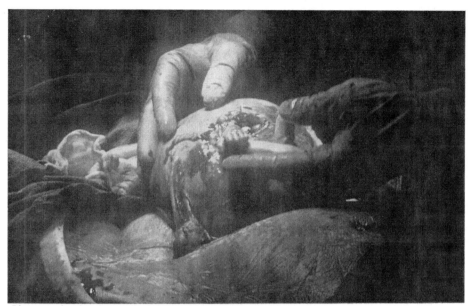

Photograph taken by Michael Clancy on August 19, 1999 in Nashville, TN. Reprinted with permission of SABA Press, New York, New York.

The tiny hand in the picture above belongs to a baby which was due to be born on December 28, 1999. The tiny hand is clutching a surgeon's finger. It is literally hanging on for life and is one of the most remarkable photographs taken in medicine. It is a record of one of the world's most extraordinary operations. The results of Samuel's surgical procedures, as revealed in Samuel's mothers' letter to the hospital, were positive. An excerpt of the letter reads as follows:

"Samuel arrived on Thursday, December 2, 1999, at 6:25pm at Northside Hospital, weighing 5 pounds, 11 ounces and measuring 20 ½ inches long. He was born at 36 weeks and did not have to spend any time in a neonatal unit and came home with his parents on Monday, December 6, 1999. Samuel's did not have any hydrocephalus and the brain malformation has resolved, as predicted by his neurosurgeon. His legs moved very well from the hips and some from the knees. He was folded in half in the womb and the orthopedist feels that he has a good chance for walking. He started physical therapy the week after going home and nursed well."

NOTES:

_____

_____

_____

_____

SALVATION (THE "REBIRTH")

Salvation is commonly referred to as the "born again" experience. The new birth takes but a moment, yet spiritual maturity takes a lifetime. *The Holy Bible* is all about salvation and redemption. In the book of John, the chapter concludes with two passages of scripture to support this premise:

And many other signs truly did Jesus in the presence of his disciples, which are not written in this book: But these are written, that ye might believe that Jesus is the Christ, the Son of God; and that believing ye might have life through his name.

—John 20:30–31 KJV

Jesus did many other miracles in the presence of his followers that are not written in this book. But these are written so that you may believe that Jesus is the Christ, the Son of God. Then, by believing, you may have life through his name.

—John 20:30–31 NCV

Jesus did many other things as well. If every one of them were written down, I suppose that even the whole world would not have room for the books that would be written.

—John 21:25 NIV

And there are also many other things which Jesus did, the which, if they should be written every one, I suppose that even the world itself could not contain the books that should be written. A-men.

—John 21:25 KJV

NOTES:

_____

_____

_____

_____

One of my favorite scriptures is found at Colossians 1:13–14 (KJV): *"Who hath delivered us from the power of darkness, and hath translated us into the kingdom of his dear Son: In whom we have redemption through his blood, even the forgiveness of sins:"* Redemption symbolizes "been set free." In the original Greek language, salvation *(sōtēria)* denotes "deliverance, preservation, salvation." Further, as used in the New Testament, salvation denotes material and temporal deliverance from danger and apprehension; spiritual and eternal deliverance granted immediately by God to those who accept His conditions of repentance and faith in the Lord Jesus, in whom alone it is to be obtained; of the present experience of God's power to deliver from the bondage of sin; and to sum up all the blessings bestowed by God on men in Christ through the Holy Spirit. As used in the English language, the word salvation (noun) is "the act of saving or state of being saved, as from harm or danger"; "deliverance from the power and penalty of sin."

Redemption (*lutroō*) denotes "to release on receipt of ransom" or "to release by paying a ransom price, to redeem." *Lutroō* signifies the actual "deliverance"—the setting at liberty. The death of Christ is stated as the means of redemption. As used in the English language, it is a noun and means "the act of redeeming or state of being redeemed."

When we pray the Prayer of Salvation (Romans 10:9 and 13), and truly mean what we pray in our hearts, God immediately forgives us of all past sins, and transfers us from the power of darkness (Satan's world system) into His glorious light. We are saved (salvaged) and redeemed from the curse of the law. We can now "see," that is, have the mental vision to perceive the honest difference between right and wrong. We should joyfully renounce the world and all of its ungodly activities while, at the same time, rejoice and praise God for His tender loving mercy.

And there is salvation in and through no one else, for there is no other name under heaven given among men by and in which we must be saved.

—Acts 4:12 Amplified

Neither is there salvation in any other: for there is no other name under heaven given among men, whereby we must be saved.

—Acts 4:12 KJV

The Word of God cuts with a two-edged sword. It cuts both ways: (1) for believers, it offers instructions on how to live a godly life (2 Timothy 3:16); and (2) for unbelievers, it brings conviction to the minds (Hebrews 4:12).

If the Son therefore shall make you free, ye should be free indeed.

—John 8:36 KJV

So if the Son makes you free, you will be truly free.

—John 8:36 NCV

NOTES:

_____

_____

_____

_____

OUR ATTITUDE TOWARD OUR "CALLING"

A changed life is the result of a changed heart.

For if there be first a willing mind, it is accepted according to that a man hath, and not according to that he hath not.

—2 Corinthians 8:12 KJV

For if the willingness is there, the gift is acceptable according to what one has, not according to what he does not have.

—2 Corinthians 8:12 NIV

NOTES:

_____

_____

_____

_____

Attitude

An attitude is an inward feeling expressed outwardly. It is defined as "our deposition or feeling toward someone or something."

A proper attitude is the start of our response process toward our calling. This became crystal clear to me one weekend during a financial workshop while I was still a relatively new member of the body of Christ. I had been saved for almost a year and a half when I witnessed a miracle before my very own eyes, on September 29 and 30, 1994. The presenter was Mr. Peter J. Daniels. Mr. Daniels is a debt-free billionaire and a native of the country of Australia. He is/was the President and Founder of the World Centre for Entrepreneurial Studies in Adelaine, South Australia. During the three sessions, he taught us the value of one's attitude. Mr. Daniels was a disadvantaged youth, plagued with illiteracy and ignorance until the age of 26. He was told by school teachers (one he actually wrote a book about named Ms. Phillips) that he would not amount to anything in life. In 1959, he heard the gospel of Jesus Christ on television while watching a Billy Graham crusade. He accepted Jesus Christ as his personal Lord and Savior as a result of that broadcast. Despite the odds that were against him as a young man, he built a large business in real estate and serves on international boards extending to the four corners of the earth. He has a no debt philosophy, is an international author of substance and quantity (nine books to his credit as of 1994), and is one of the world's higher paid public speakers (usual fee is $100,000 per engagement). He books over 200 air flights annually to fulfill schedules and endeavors to meet any genuine need.

Mr. Daniel's primary intent was to teach on the subject of finance, and he did. However, the recurring theme that would surface time and time again was *attitude*. He spent considerable time discussing principles for entrepreneurship and attitude. The expression, "Your Attitude Determines Your Altitude," became expressly clear to me during that weekend. The following principles concerning attitude were extracted from his intensive and thought-provoking seminar/workshop.

Table 4. Principles for Entrepreneurship & Attitude

Mastery of procrastination	**"Do it now!"**
Enthusiasm	
Develop habit force	**Change your life by changing your habits**
Develop a positive mental attitude	**Focus on how things can be done**
Pay the full price	Commitment to excellence; READ! The brain is like a tank with a slow leak; know your stuff!
Learn the art of speaking on your feet	
Handle your emotions	Emotion is not subject to reason, but to action
Criticism	**There is no power in criticism except the power that you give it**
The Law of Attraction	You don't get a second chance to make a first impression
Persistence	
How do you handle worry?	**Worry is creating mental pictures of the things that we don't want; instead, create mental pictures of the things that we do want**
Learn to make decisions	**Successful people make decisions quickly and change them rarely. Conversely, unsuccessful people make decisions s-l-o-w-l-y and change them often...**
Save Money	
Be in charge of every conversation	Ask the questions
Failure principles	Winning of souls; no illicit sex
Power of CHOICE	

Bold *references are attitudinal.*

Desire to succeed in life begins with your attitude. Your desire must be married to your purpose, then add faith, perseverance, and a thankful heart. This is how to turn desire into manifestation:

A Five-Part Affirmation for Success

1. I know exactly what I want.
2. I want it sincerely.
3. I know that it is mine.
4. I exert every possible effort to obtain it.
5. I now give thanks, knowing what I desire is mine to enjoy.

AND SO IT IS![7]

We can understand God's Word

Understanding God's Word requires readiness and an act of our will (attitude). There are two words in the original Greek language that best describe this concept:

Ginōskō—to allow oneself to learn, and

Manthanō—to understand learning.

Used together, they have a tri-fold meaning:
- ✓ to allow oneself to increase in knowledge;
- ✓ to learn by use and practice; and
- ✓ to allow understanding by an act of one's will.

Accept, I beseech thee, the freewill offerings of my mouth, O LORD, and teach me thy judgments.

—Psalm 119:108 KJV

Accept, I pray, the freewill offerings of my mouth, O LORD, And teach me Your judgments.

—Psalm 119:108 NKJV

Help me understand the meaning of your commandments, and I will meditate on your wonderful deeds.

—Psalm 119:27 NLT

Make me to understand the way of thy precepts: so shall I talk of thy wondrous works.

—Psalm 119:27 KJV

Give me understanding, and I shall keep thy law; yea, I shall observe it with my whole heart.

—Psalm 119:34 KJV

Help me understand, so I can keep your teachings, obeying them with all my heart.

—Psalm 119:34 NCV

Your hands made me and formed me; give me understanding to learn your commands.

—Psalm 119:73 NIV

Thy hands have made me and fashioned me: give me understanding, that I may learn thy commandments.

—Psalm 119:73 KJV

I am Your servant; give me understanding (discernment and comprehension), that I may know (discern and be familiar with the character of) Your testimonies.

—Psalm 119:125 Amplified

I am thy servant; give me understanding, that I may know thy testimonies.

—Psalm 119:125 KJV

NOTES:

_____

_____

_____

_____

With a proper attitude, God's Word will direct, encourage, satisfy, and guide us. The psalmist wrote these comforting passages of scripture in chapter 119:

Psalm 119:105   God's Word lights our path;
Psalm 119:106–109   Instruction on how to please God;
Psalm 119:110   God's Word encourages us in affliction;
Psalm 119:111   God's Word helps us not to stray from His Word (truth); and
Psalm 119:112   God's Word gives us joy.

NOTES:

_____

_____

_____

_____

> ## TIME VALUE(S)

See then that ye walk circumspectly, not as fools, but as wise, Redeeming the time, because the days are evil.

—Ephesians 5:15–16 KJV

So be careful how you live. Don't live like fools, but like those who are wise. Make the most of every opportunity in these evil days.

—Ephesians 5:15–16 NLT

Management of Time

Time: Use it or lose it. It is one of the few commodities on earth that once lost, it cannot be regained. Each day consists of:

- ✓ 86,400 seconds;
- ✓ 1,440 minutes; and
- ✓ 24 hours.

Each week consists of:

- ✓ 604,800 seconds;
- ✓ 10,080 minutes; and
- ✓ 168 hours.

Each month consists of:

- ✓ 2,419,200 seconds;
- ✓ 40,320 minutes; and
- ✓ 672 hours.

Each year consists of:

- ✓ 29,030,400 seconds;
- ✓ 483,840 minutes; and
- ✓ 8,064 hours.

What's the point? The point is that we are allotted the exact same amount of time each and every day. Either we value it and treat it as a valued treasure. Or we abuse or otherwise waste it. Our failure to maximize our time hampers our ability to effectively manage our calling. Every area of our lives is tied, in one way or another, to our management—or mismanagement—of time. Prioritization of important, urgent, and critical milestones become increasingly vital to our overall effectiveness in life. It can even be viewed as a key barometer for success and failure.

NOTES:

_____

_____

_____

_____

Sleep

God's Word provides detailed and clear instructions relative to proper rest, getting enough sleep, and maintaining a high energy level.

It is useless for you to work so hard from early morning until late at night, anxiously working for food to eat; for God gives rest to his loved ones.

—Psalm 127:2 NLT

It is vain for you to rise up early, to sit up late, to eat the bread of sorrows: for so he giveth his beloved sleep.

—Psalm 127:2 KJV

I will lie down and sleep in peace, for you alone, O LORD, make me dwell in safety.

—Psalm 4:8 NIV

I will both lay me down in peace, and sleep: for thou LORD, only makest me dwell in safety.

—Psalm 4:8 KJV

When thou liest down, thou shalt not be afraid: yea, thou shalt lie down, and thy sleep shall be sweet.

—Proverbs 3:24 KJV

When you lie down, you will not be afraid; Yes, you will lie down and your sleep will be sweet.

—Proverbs 3:24 NKJV

He giveth power to the faint; and to them that have no might he increaseth strength. Even the youths shall faint and be weary, and the young men shall utterly fall: But they that wait upon the LORD shall renew their strength; they shall mount up with wings as eagles; they shall run, and not be weary; and they shall walk, and not faint.

—Isaiah 40:29–31 KJV

He gives strength to those who are tired and more power to those who are weak. Even children become tired and need to rest, and young people trip and fall. But the people who trust the LORD will become strong again. They will rise up as an eagle in the sky; they will run and not need rest; they will walk and not become tired.

—Isaiah 40:29–31 NCV

On October 16, 2000, the *U.S. News and World Report* released a cover page story entitled, "Sleepless Society: In staying up half the night, we may risk our health." The article hits hard in the very opening paragraph:

> *Americans are loath to say good night to responsibilities and fun. Job and family beckon. Late-night television entices. The Internet seduces. Supermarkets and megastores lure shoppers well into the wee hours. By the millions, we succumb to the temptations of the night. Each weekday night we get an hour and six minutes less, on average, than the eight hours that sleep experts recommend, each weekend night half an hour less. By the end of the year, we are short 338 hours - two full weeks - of rest. We are the great unslept, somnambulating through life on the verge of sleep bankruptcy.*

It is no secret that sleep deprivation causes a lack of awareness and attention to detail. In 1999, it is estimated that American citizens racked up a cumulative national sleep debt of 105 billion hours. David Dingis, director of experimental psychiatry at the University of Pennsylvania School of Medicine said, "Sleep resettles us emotionally, cognitively, and immunologically. It's just good." Preliminary studies by sleep researchers indicate that a lack of sleep contributes to a decline in immune function. Further, it changes white blood cell counts and immune response modifiers, biological evidence that the body is having trouble fighting infection.

Other solutions can become clearer to people who get adequate rest. We can sleep in peace when we remember that God is awake.

NOTES:

_____

_____

_____

_____

It is time to decide

Your vocation, and the answers related to it belong to you, are meant for you, like a perfect love or soul mate. Yet often we play a kind of adult hide-and-seek before finding (or inventing) our vocation.[8] Think of time as money and be frugal with both.[9]

In a comprehensive article that was featured in *Parade* magazine,[10] Lyric Wallwork Winik writes about "When the Call Comes Later in Life." At least half of all the men and women that answer their calling into the ministry do so after the age of 35. The lives of six men and women are chronicled, and include an attorney, entertainment executive, computer specialist, radio journalist, banker, and an actress. Ted Schmitt, the former Universal Studios entertainment executive (Senior Vice President), made a decision to answer his calling at age 54 when Home Entertainment was the biggest moneymaker of all of the studio's divisions. He is quoted as saying "Problems hit, family members died. It makes you evaluate what life is. Is it corporate quarterly profits or something more? I didn't think that I had the ability not to be selfish, not to worry about money and things, but those things aren't important."

While we recommit ourselves to our calling, the concept of fasting deserves special attention and consideration. Fasting has a spiritual purpose, and that purpose is to get your flesh out of the way so that the Spirit of God can move in your life. Fasting removes the barriers to communication with God and allows the spirit man to commune directly with the heavenly Father without disturbance. Most of us who live comfortably in the prosperous nations have problems with prayer and fasting because everything around us is designed to appeal to our flesh and its carnal desires. But when we seek the face of God through prayer and fasting, we push the flesh aside, denying the appetites and the control they seek over us, and allowing our spirit man, who desires God, to develop a strong relationship with the heavenly Father.

Man is a triune being made up of the body, soul, and spirit. It is the spirit that came from God and desires to be reunited with God. Given the opportunity, the spirit will reach out to God and communicate with Him. Because Christ is our Lord and Savior and because we are totally dependent on Him, it is of utmost importance that we know His will at any given time. To know the will of God, it is necessary to live close to Him and to hear His voice. Prayer and fasting makes you sensitive to the voice of the Lord. It enables you to hear Him above the sound of other voices around you. What could be more important?[11]

Pray your day and walk the way that you pray!

Do not be anxious about anything, but in everything, by prayer and petition, with thanksgiving, present your requests to God. And the peace of God, which transcends all understanding, will guard your hearts and your minds in Christ Jesus. Finally, brothers, whatever is true, whatever is noble, whatever is right, whatever is pure, whatever is lovely, whatever is admirable—if anything is excellent or praiseworthy—think about such things. Whatever you have learned or received or heard from me, or seen in me—put it into practice. And the God of peace will be with you.

—Philippians 4:6–9 NIV

Be careful for nothing; but in every thing by prayer and supplication with thanksgiving let your requests be known unto God. And the peace of God, which passeth all understanding, shall keep your hearts and minds through Christ Jesus. Finally, brethen, whatsoever things are true, whatsoever things are honest, whatsoever things are just, whatsoever things are pure, whatsoever things are lovely, whatsoever things are of good report; if there be any virtue, and if there be any praise, think on these things. Those things, which ye have both learned, and received, and heard, and seen in me, do: and the God of peace shall be with you.

—Philippians 4:6–9 KJV

NOTES:

_____

_____

_____

_____

STUDY QUESTIONS AND DISCUSSION

Chapter Two

1.   Do you know why you were birthed into the earth? (Deuteronomy 6:1)

_____

_____

_____

2.   What is *your* calling? (1 Peter 3:9)

_____

_____

_____

3.   Are you currently fulfilling your divine purpose?

_____

_____

_____

4.   Your divine assignment awaits you. Do you know what it is?

_____

_____

_____

5.   What steps will you take today to "reconnect" to God? (2 Corinthians 2:14)

_____

_____

_____

Chapter Three

Knowing Your Spiritual Gift(s)

God has established in our hearts certain *gifts* which are operational within the earth-realm. These twenty (20) gifts are categorized as power or protection (operational), functional and perfecting. These 20 gifts work in unison with the nine fruit of the Spirit (Galatians 5:22–23). The Word of God operates through us, as predestined before the Earth was formed, based upon the gift(s) that God has entrusted to us. To be fully used by God, we must know and understand our gifts in order to maximize our productivity in the Kingdom of God. In doing so, we also raise the level of productivity of those who are within our sphere of influence.

For to one is given by the Spirit the word of wisdom; to another the word of knowledge by the same Spirit; To another faith by the same Spirit; to another the gifts of healing by the same Spirit; To another the working of miracles; to another prophecy; to another discerning of spirits; to another divers kinds of tongues; to another the interpretation of tongues: But all these worketh that one and the selfsame Spirit, dividing to every man severally as he will.

—1 Corinthians 12:8–11 KJV

Having then gifts differing according to the grace that is given to us, whether prophecy, let us prophesy according to the proportion of faith; Or ministry, let us wait on our ministering: or he teacheth, on teaching; Or he that exhorteth, on exhortation: he that giveth, let him do it with simplicity; he that ruleth, with diligence; he that shewth mercy, with cheerfulness.

—Romans 12:6–8 KJV

Wherefore he saith, WHEN HE ASCENDED UP ON HIGH, HE LED CAPTIVITY CAPTIVE, AND GAVE GIFTS UNTO MEN. And he gave some, apostles; and some, prophets; and some, evangelists; and some, pastors and teachers; For the perfecting of the saints, for the work of the ministry, for the edifying of the body of Christ:

—Ephesians 4: 8 and 11–12 KJV (emphasis added)

*T*o know God is to glorify Him through our *gift(s)*. The unique gift(s) that each of us possess were given to us freely by God so that we may fulfill our purpose in the earth. Our divine purpose, the ultimate reason that we were birthed into the world, will become fruitful and we will raise the level of productivity of others (those within our sphere of influence), by utilizing the gifts(s) that God has entrusted us with. First, we must know what the spiritual gifts are prior to coming into knowledge of how to utilize them.

In this chapter, God clearly illustrates how He is glorified through the working of our gifts and how they tie into the nine fruits of the Spirit. The three (3) categories of spiritual gifts are:

- ✓ Operational gifts (by the will of the Spirit to protect or empower),
- ✓ Functional gifts (by the will of man toward society), and
- ✓ Perfecting gifts (by the will of man to develop maturity).

Central Theme: Using your gift(s) to maximize your productivity.
Keyword: Gift(s)

"Gift" defined:
   Dōrea (New Testament)—denotes a "free gift," stressing its gratuitous character. It is always used in the New Testament of a spiritual or supernatural gift. Examples include John 4:10, Acts 8:20 and 11:17,

Romans 5:15, 2 Corinthians 9:15, Ephesians 3:7, and Hebrews 6:4. In Ephesians 4:7, "according to the measure of the gift of Christ," the "gift" is that given by Christ. In Acts 2:28, "the gift of the Holy Ghost," the clause is epexegetical, the "gift" being the Holy Ghost himself.

This free gift is never taken away by God. It is either used or not used to glorify God. It is up to each of us to utilize our gifts as we fulfill our purpose for being birthed into the earth.

For God's gifts and his call are irrevocable.

—Romans 11:29 NIV

For the gifts and calling of God are without repentance.

—Romans 11:29 KJV

OPERATIONAL GIFTS

To one is given in and through the [Holy] Spirit [the power to speak] a message of wisdom, and to another [the power to express] a word of knowledge and understanding according to the same [Holy] Spirit; To another [wonder-working] faith by the same [Holy] Spirit, to another the extraordinary powers of healing by the one Spirit; To another the working of miracles, to another prophetic insight (the gift of interpreting the divine will and purpose); to another the ability to discern and distinguish between [the utterances of true] spirits [and false ones], to another various kinds of [unknown] tongues, to another the ability to interpret [such] tongues. All these [gifts, achievements, abilities] are inspired and brought to pass by one and the same [Holy] Spirit, Who apportions to each person individually [exactly] as He chooses.

—1 Corinthians 12:8–11 Amplified

For to one is given by the Spirit the word of wisdom; to another the word of knowledge by the same Spirit; To another faith by the same Spirit; to another the gifts of healing by the same Spirit; To another the working of miracles; to another prophecy; to another discerning of spirits; to another divers kinds of tongues; to another the interpretation of tongues: But all these worketh that one and the selfsame Spirit, dividing to every man severally as he will.

—1 Corinthians 12:8–11 KJV

Through the will of the Spirit, 1 Corinthians 12:8–10 identifies the nine protection or power gifts. These gifts protect and empower you and I to do the will of God concerning our lives. These gifts are manifested through our words, our acts, and what we know. God is glorified through the operation of these gifts in the natural realm. That is, they can be seen of men. They are as follows:

Wisdom, Knowledge, Faith, Healing, Miracles, Prophecy, Discerning of spirits, Divers kinds of tongues, and Interpretation of tongues

<u>Gift (*Hebrew or Greek word*)—Original meaning in Hebrew or Greek</u>

Wisdom (*phronēsis*): understanding; prudence.

Knowledge (i. *proginōskō*, ii. *epiginōskō*, iii. *ginōskō*)
i.   to know the truth before hand
ii.   a perception of the truth; to be very detailed and knowledgable to a particular subject
iii.   to come to know, understand, and accept fully while walking in progressional knowledge

Faith (*pistis*)—the ability to discern modes of action with a view to their results; firm persuasion. In Hebrews 11:1, "the substance of things hoped for, the evidence of things not seen."

Healing [*iama* (noun)/*iaomai* (verb)]—a means of healing; a healing (the result of the act); to heal of physical treatment (used 22 times). Luke, the physician, used the word 15 times.

Miracles (*sēmēion*)—"a sign, mark, token"; it is used of "miracles" and wonders as signs of divine authority.

Prophecy (*prophēteia*)—speaking forth of the mind and counsel of God.

Discerning of spirits (*anakrinō*)—to distinguish or separate out as to investigate (*krin*) by looking throughout (*ana*) objects or particulars. Also means to examine, scrutinize, question, to hold a preliminary judicial examination preceding the trial proper.

Divers kinds of tongues [*diaphorôs* (adjective)]—varying in kind; different; diverse.

Interpretation of tongues (*epilusis*)—"to loose, solve, or explain"; denotes a solution or explanation. For example, in 2 Peter 1:20, the writers of scripture did not put their own construction upon the "God-breathed" words they wrote.

NOTES:

_____

_____

_____

_____

Upon further examination of 1 Corinthians 12, the Apostle Paul provides in-depth instruction and counsel on the principles of exercising spiritual gifts. His purpose for this instruction is so that you and I would not be ignorant; ignorant relative to the operation of the spiritual gifts (verse 1). Further, Paul's instruction reminds us of how we used to follow the advice of lifeless idols, but now, as converted Christians, no man can say that Jesus is Lord but by the Holy Spirit (verses 2 and 3).

There are many, or different, gifts but the same (one) Spirit. Likewise, there are different ministries, but the same Lord. There are also various kinds of activities, but it is the same God who works in us all (verses 4–6). The key to Paul's instruction lies with verse 7: The manifestation of the Spirit is given to every one for the benefit of others. Each of the nine operational gifts work interchangeably within the same Spirit, assigned individually to each of us.

Now, as members of the body of Christ, God has placed "some" in the church for the purpose of manifesting our gifts for the benefit of others. First apostles, secondly prophets, and thirdly teachers, then miracles, gifts of healings, helps, governments, and diversities of tongues (verse 28). The operative word is "some," because everyone will not have the gifts of the apostle, or the prophet, or the teacher. God admonishes each of us, however, to respect and use the gift(s) that He has freely given unto us and that He will show us a more excellent way (verse 31).

NOTES:

_____

_____

_____

_____

FUNCTIONAL GIFTS

Having then gifts differing according to the grace that is given to us, whether prophecy, let us prophesy according to the proportion of faith; Or ministry, let us wait on our ministering: or he teacheth, on teaching; Or he that exhorteth, on exhortation: he that giveth, let him do it with simplicity; he that ruleth, with diligence; he that shewth mercy, with cheerfulness.

—Romans 12:6–8 KJV

We have different gifts, according to the grace given us. If a man's gift is prophesying, let him use it in proportion to his faith. If it is serving, let him serve; if it is teaching, let him teach; if it is encouraging, let him encourage; if it is contributing to the needs of others, let him give generously; if it is leadership, let him govern diligently; if it is showing mercy, let him do it cheerfully.

—Romans 12:6–8 NIV

Through the will (choice) of man, Romans 12:6–8 identifies the seven (7) functional gifts. Functional gifts specifically identify our responsibilities toward society and one another in the body of Christ. How we conduct our everyday affairs in the presence of people who have no relationship with God (verse 20), as well as the brothers and sisters in Christ (verse 13), is taught in this scripture. The functional gifts are:

Prophesy (encouragement by the measure of faith),
Ministry (service with patience),
Exhortation (wise counsel),
Teaching (instruction),

Giving (giving without complicating matters—simplicity is key),
Ruling (diligent leadership), and
Showing mercy (cheerful compassion).

Gift (*Hebrew or Greek word*)—Original meaning in Hebrew or Greek

Prophesy (*prophetēia*)—speaking forth the mind and counsel of God. The declaration of that which cannot be known by natural means (the foretelling of the will of God whether with reference to past, present, or future).

Ministry (*diakonia*)—service; servant of the Lord in preaching and teaching.

Exhortation (*paraklēsis*)—a calling to one's side; to one's aid; consolation and comfort.

Teaching (*didaskalia*)—that which is taught; doctrine; instruction; learning. Occurs fifteen times in the New Testament.

Giving (*charizomai*)—"to show favor or kindness"; to give freely, bestow graciously. Refers mostly to what is "given" by God.

Ruling (*proistēmi*)—to stand before, to lead, attend to (indicating care and diligence). Is translated "to rule" (middle voice), with reference to a local church.

Showing mercy (*eleos*)—the outward manifestation of pity.

NOTES:

_____

_____

_____

_____

Upon further examination of the twelfth chapter of Romans, the Apostle Paul instructs us on proper responsibilities toward the society in which we live. Beginning in verse 3, he reminds us that through the grace that has been given by God, we are to be humble and not think too highly of ourselves. This is applicable to all situations and circumstances in life. As God has dealt to all men, and women, the measure of faith, we are commanded to exercise our gift(s) with humility and in faith. Paul's purpose for this instruction is so that you and I would be mindful that each of the seven functional spiritual gifts have a different benefit within the body of Christ, yet we are one body in Christ and each of us are members one of another (verses 4–6).

As we function together as one, in love which is the overriding theme, it becomes much less challenging to apply God's Word to our daily lives. In verses 9–21, you and I are specifically instructed to love, serve, extend kindness, be instant in prayer, be honest, serve the Lord, overcome evil with good, live peaceably with all men, and not seek revenge. These instructions apply to all situations and to all of God's people. The blessings of Gods' functional gift(s) allows us to remain in obedience to His Word. Circumstances and situations shall not prevail, but the Word of God shall prevail in your life.

NOTES:

_____

_____

_____

_____

PERFECTING GIFTS

Wherefore he saith, WHEN HE ASCENDED UP ON HIGH, HE LED CAPTIVITY CAPTIVE, AND GAVE GIFTS UNTO MEN. And he gave some, apostles; and some, prophets; and some, evangelists; and some, pastors and teachers; For the perfecting of the saints, for the work of the ministry, for the edifying of the body of Christ:

—Ephesians 4:8 and 11–12 KJV (emphasis added)

Therefore He says: "When He ascended on high, He led captivity captive, And gave gifts to men." And He Himself gave some to be apostles, some prophets, some evangelists, and some pastors and teachers, for the equipping of the saints for the work of ministry, for the edifying of the body of Christ.

—Ephesians 4:8 and 11–12 NKJV

Through the will (choice) of man, Ephesians 4:11 identifies the four perfecting gifts. These gifts are designed to "perfect" you and I. "Perfect," in this instance, does not refer to something without a flaw. God has called into the ministry those that can preach and teach His Word in a manner that will cause growth, development, and maturity to those of us with an ear to hear. These perfecting gifts are as follows:

Apostles, Prophets, Evangelists, and Pastors and Teachers

Gift *(Hebrew or Greek word)*—Original meaning in Hebrew or Greek

Apostles (*apostolos*)— "one sent forth" (describes Jesus' relation to God).
Prophets (*prophētēs*)—one who speaks forth or openly; a proclaimer of a divine message. For example, in the Old Testament, the prophet's messages were very largely the proclamation of the divine purposes of salvation and glory to be accomplished in the future.

Evangelists (*euangelistēs*)—a messenger of good; preacher of the gospel.

i. Pastors <u>and</u> ii. Teachers (i. *poimēn*; ii. *kalodidaskalos*)—i. a shepherd; one who tends herds and flocks. Pastors guide as well as feed the flock.; ii. A teacher of what is good.

God's leaders in the ministry are called for a purpose. That is, to "perfect" (bring to maturity) all of His people relative to His Word. Verse 12 sums it up:*"For the perfecting of the saints."* Further, the verse adds that these leaders are called, *"For the work of the ministry and for the edifying of the body of Christ."* Edifying refers to "building up." These leaders are commanded to preach and teach until we all come into the unity of faith and the knowledge of Jesus Christ (verse 13) and until we are "perfected."

Upon further study of verses 14 and 15, the purpose of the perfecting gifts are to instruct us in correct biblical knowledge so that our maturity will eliminate a tendency to follow whatever the latest religious movement may be offering. Being firm in the doctrine of Jesus Christ, we will not be led away by tricks and gimmicks that may sound or look good, but have no biblical foundation.

NOTES:

_____

_____

_____

_____

FRUIT OF THE SPIRIT

(For the fruit of the Spirit is in all goodness and righteousness and truth;) Proving what is acceptable unto the Lord. And have no fellowship with the unfruitful works of darkness, but rather reprove them. For it is a shame even to speak of those things which are done of them in secret.

—Ephesians 5:9–12 KJV

(for the fruit of the light consists in all goodness, righteousness and truth) and find out what pleases the Lord. Have nothing to do with the fruitless deeds of darkness, but rather expose them. For it is shameful even to mention what the disobedient do in secret.

—Ephesians 5:9–12 NIV

Through spiritual growth, we all display an outward manifestation of the fruit (which literally means growth) of the Spirit. In Galatians 5:22–23, the nine characteristics of fruit are identified as follows:

> *Love* (unconditional love),
> *Joy* (delight; elation; gladness),
> *Peace* (internal serenity),
> *Longsuffering* (patience),
> *Gentleness* (caring),
> *Goodness* (kindheartedness),
> *Faith* (faithfulness),
> *Meekness* (power under control—the opposite of weakness), and
> *Temperance* (self-control).

Fruit (*Hebrew or Greek word*)—Original meaning in Hebrew or Greek

Love (*agapē*)—Christian love, whether exercised toward the brethen, or toward men generally, is not an impulse from the feelings, it does not always run with the natural inclinations, nor does it spend itself only upon those for whom some affinity is discovered. Love seeks the welfare of all and works no ill to any; love seeks opportunity to do good to all men, and "especially toward them that are of the household of faith" (Galatians 6:10).

Joy (*chairē*)—to rejoice; be glad.

Peace (*eirēnē*)—the sense of rest and contentment consequent thereon; harmonious relationships between men; friendliness.

Longsuffering (*makrothumēo*)—forbearance; patience; to bear with.

Gentleness (*epiekeia*)—denotes "fairness, moderation, gentleness"; sweet reasonableness. Considers the ideas of equity and justice, which are essential to the original meaning.

Goodness (*agathōsunē*)—moral quality which is described by the adjective "agathos." Being good in its character or constitution; is beneficial in its effect.

Faith (*pistis*)—the ability to discern modes of action with a view to their results; firm persuasion. In Hebrews 11:1, "the substance of things hoped for, the evidence of things not seen."

Meekness (*praütēs*)—power under control.

Temperance (*enkrateia*)—control of self.

NOTES:

_____

_____

_____

_____

Perhaps the most important message relative to the fruit of the Spirit is found in Galations 5:23, "*there is no law.*" No government can legislate love, gentleness, temperance, nor goodness. A law cannot be enacted that will make anyone become a kinder and gentler person. These are gifts that come from God and are accessed when we make a conscious decision to reconnect to Him.

As members of the body of Christ, God instructs and commands us to walk (live) after the spirit and not the flesh. The works of the flesh include many ungodly activities such as adultery, fornication, lust, uncleanness, witchcraft, strife, hatred, divisions, jealousy, envying, murder, drunkenness. The Lord even goes on to state that *things such like these* are included although not specifically referenced in the scripture (verse 19–21). Notice that each of these negative attributes is contrary to the fruit of the Spirit listed above. They are characteristic of what the flesh wants to do. By the grace of God, we are no longer subjected to behaving in such a way that dishonors Him. By His grace, we can exhibit love, joy, peace, longsuffering (suffering a long time for Christ's sake), gentleness, goodness, faithfulness, meekness, and temperance (self control), in spite of our circumstances. By walking after the spirit, as we are commanded to do, God's Word says that we shall not fulfill the lust of the flesh (verse 16). In our relationship to Christ, Jesus speaks to us in the fifteenth chapter of John, saying, "I am the vine, ye are the branches: He that abideth in me, and I in him, the same bringeth forth much fruit: for without me ye can do nothing" (John 15:5).

In the book entitled, *How to Think like a CEO: The 22 Vital Traits you need to be the Person at the Top,* the author describes the chief executive officer (CEO) as a person that requires eight essential qualities, or elements, to be successful at his/her level within any given corporation.

The chief who constantly works on developing personal power rather than relying on position power is doing his/her job. Really effective power does not come from title or money, but character. The CEO has real power if he/she has the following:

>   patience,
>   calmness,
>   forbearance,
>   ability,
>   energy,
>   sympathy,
>   spirit, and
>   ethics.[12]

Notice how a climb up the corporate ladder emulates God's Word concerning the spiritual gifts and the fruit of the Spirit. The business world recognizes that it is necessary to possess some moral qualities as one strives to the office of CEO. For the CEO, and those that aspire to that office within a corporation, understand the importance of relationships and the proper temperament required to be successful at that level. God requires the same level of commitment for His children. You may not aspire to become a CEO, but God promises in His Word that if we acknowledge our gift, which was given to us by Him, then He will promote us to even higher heights than the office of CEO. God will strategically place us before men and women that will promote our efforts and cause us to make optimum use of our gift.

> *This is why I remind you to keep using the gift God gave you when I laid my hands on you. Now let it grow, as a small flame grows into a fire.*
>
> —2 Timothy 1:6 NCV

> *Wherefore I put thee in remembrance that thou stir up the gift of God, which is in thee by the putting on of my hands.*
>
> —2 Timothy 1:6 KJV

> *A man's gift maketh room for him, and bringeth him before great men.*
>
> —Proverbs 18:16 KJV

> *A gift opens the way for the giver and ushers him into the presence of the great.*
>
> —Proverbs 18:16 NIV

NOTES:

_____

_____

_____

_____

STUDY QUESTIONS AND DISCUSSION

Chapter Three

1.   What gift(s) has God freely given unto you?

_____

_____

_____

2.   Will you use it/them to glorify Him? (2 Timothy 1:6)

_____

_____

_____

3.   Without God, you cannot operate in the fruit of the Spirit. Will you trust Him today, obey His Word and bear fruit?

_____

_____

_____

4.   Ask God to reveal your gift(s) to you. Will you do it now? (Matthew 21:21–22)

_____

_____

_____

5.   Will you glorify God by working diligently to perfect your gift(s)? (1 Timothy 4:14)

_____

_____

_____

Part II — DO THE WILL OF GOD

*Hereby perceive we the love of God, because he laid down his life for us: and we ought to lay down our lives for the brethren. But whoso hath this world's good, and seeth his brother have need, and shutteth up his bowels of compassion from him, how dwelleth the love of God in him? My little children, let us not love in word, neither in tongue; but in deed and in truth. And hereby we know that we are of the truth, and shall assure our hearts before him. For if our heart condemn us, God is greater than our heart, and knoweth all things. Beloved, if our heart condemn us not, then we have confidence toward God. And whatsoever we ask, we receive of him, because we keep his commandments, and **do those things that are pleasing in his sight**.*

—1 John 3:16–22 KJV (emphasis added)

*This is how we know what love is: Jesus Christ laid down his life for us. And we ought to lay down our lives for our brothers. If anyone has material possessions and sees his brother in need but has no pity on him, how can the love of God be in him? Dear children, let us not love with words or tongue but with actions and in truth. This then is how we know that we belong to the truth, and how we set our hearts at rest in his presence whenever our hearts condemn us. For God is greater than our hearts, and he knows everything. Dear friends, if our hearts do not condemn us, we have confidence before God and receive from him anything we ask, because **we obey his commands and do what pleases him**.*

—1 John 3:16–22 NIV (emphasis added)

Chapter Four

Spread the Gospel!

Christians are compelled to tell and/or show others of the "good news" of Jesus Christ. We are commanded to do so, but there should be a yearning in the heart to do so nonetheless. This can be accomplished through our lifestyle, inviting others to church, and ministering to others during a low point in their lives.

For unto us a child is born, unto us a son is given: and the government shall be upon his shoulder: and his name shall be called Wonderful, Counsellor, The mighty God, The everlasting Father, The Prince of Peace. Of the increase of his government and peace there shall be no end, upon the throne of David, and upon his kingdom, to order it, and to establish it with judgment and with justice from henceforth even for ever. The zeal of the Lord of hosts will perform this.

—Isaiah 9:6–7 KJV

Go ye therefore, and teach all nations, baptizing them in the name of the Father, and of the Son, and of the Holy Ghost: Teaching them to observe all things whatsoever I have commanded you: and, lo, I am with you alway, even unto the end of the world. A-men

—Matthew 28:19–20 KJV

*T*o do the will of God, we glorify Him by *spreading the gospel* (good news). The good news of Jesus is spread through human agents: you and I. We represent Jesus Christ in the earth realm and are commanded to carry His message of salvation and redemption throughout the uttermost parts of the world. If we do not accept this mandate, God cannot be glorified. Neither can the Body of Christ be edified.

When I accepted Jesus Christ as my personal Lord and Savior, I felt an immediate change in both my physical body and my mind (soul). Objects appeared different. Trees and grass appeared to be greener. I began to see other people the way that God sees them—as His children. Within just a few weeks, it was quite easy for me to proclaim His name, because of my personal victories. Since I was no longer lost, alienated, and shut off from God, it became so easy to spread the good news to everyone around me—friends, co-workers, bosses, and even in our annual family Christmas newsletter.

In this chapter, God reminds us how to know Him by doing His will. His will is that we come into the knowledge of truth, accept the gift of salvation through redemption, and lead others to Christ. We should display an overwhelming desire to see others have access to God—to reconcile others to God. He demonstrates in four ways how we can spread the gospel. They are through:

- ✓ Personal relationships—an examination of the book of Romans,
- ✓ Ambassadors for Christ—how we should represent Christ on earth, and
- ✓ There's a large audience out there—everyone is your neighbor.

Central Theme: Tell others about the good news of Jesus Christ.
Keyword: Gospel

"Gospel" defined:

Euangelion (New Testament)—is a noun meaning "to preach." Originally denoted as a reward for good tidings. Later, the idea of reward dropped and the word stood for the good news itself. The English word gospel, that is, "good message," is the equivalent of *euangelion* (English version of evangel). In the New Testament, it denotes the good tidings of the kingdom of God and of salvation through Jesus

Christ, to be received by faith, on the basis of His expiatory (to make amends for) death, burial, resurrection, and ascension, as confirmed in Acts 15:7 and 20:24, and 1 Peter 4:17.

PERSONAL RELATIONSHIPS

Romans' Gospel Message: The Good News of Jesus Christ

It is a message about personal relationships[13] and practical exhortation: *Jesus Christ is more than just facts to be believed—It is also a life to be lived.* The message is for everybody. It was designed by God to be meaningful and applicable to every person on earth, without regard to where they live, who they are, or the culture (geographic boundaries) in which they were raised.

The book of *Romans* is an epistle (letter) written by Paul the Apostle to the Romans approximately fifty-seven years after the death and ascension of Jesus Christ. It is considered Paul's greatest work and is placed first among his thirteen epistles in the New Testament. Paul was born a Jew in the city of Tarsus; he was a Roman citizen, tentmaker, and a Pharisee, responsible for the persecution of Christians before his conversion on the road to Damascus. He became a faithful follower of Christ, a dedicated missionary, and a respected leader in the early church. The book of Romans explores the significance of Christ's sacrificial death, whereas the four Gospels (Matthew, Luke, Mark and John) represent the words and works of Jesus Christ. During the time of the writing, the city of Rome was the greatest city in the world with over one million inhabitants, yet the majority were slaves.

The key words throughout this book are righteousness, faith, law, all, and sin. Each appear at least sixty times. Jesus Christ is presented as the Second Adam whose righteousness and substitutionary death have provided for all who place their faith in Him.

Paul's message concerning personal relationships is immediately captured in verse 7 of the first chapter of Romans; His message is written to those called saints (believers in Christ) in Rome. Paul, himself, establishes a personal relationship with the readers of his message in verses 9 through 13 through a series of key messages:

- ✓ Making mention of them repeatedly, to God, in his prayers;
- ✓ By the will of God, he is coming to the Romans to deliver a message;
- ✓ Shares with the Romans some spiritual gift (the gifts and calling of God are without repentance—11:29);
- ✓ Desires to be comforted together by the mutual faith that they share; and
- ✓ Comes to them so that they will not be ignorant and to share some fruit even as he did amongst the Gentiles.

Paul admonishes the Romans throughout this book to recognize and live according to the righteousness of God. That is, how it is revealed and how to apply it to their lives. In Chapter 2, verse 10 reminds the Romans that *"There is none righteous, no, not one."* In Chapter 3, Paul proves that all humankind has sinned. The key words used during his instruction are "coming short," "unrighteousness," "trespass," "iniquity," "transgression," and "ungodliness." Each of these descriptions, according to Paul, interferes with our ability to establish and maintain personal relationships with humankind. Chapter 12 is perhaps the operative chapter in Romans as it relates to establishing and maintaining personal relationships with mankind. Responsibilities toward God and toward society are specifically addressed.

As it relates to God, we are instructed not to be conformed to this world's system, but to be transformed with the renewing of our mind and to present our bodies a living sacrifice, holy, acceptable unto God (verse 1 and 2). In other words, the least that we can do is to conform to the kingdom standards that are clearly established in Jesus' trial discourse (Sermon on the Mount), Matthew chapters 5, 6, and 7. Do not rely on the world's system, but God's kingdom standards. As it relates to society, Paul instructs us to be humble, remove all hidden agendas, promote honesty, live peaceably with all men, if possible, and to overcome evil with good.

NOTES:

_____

_____

_____

AMBASSADORS FOR CHRIST

The gospel (good news of Jesus Christ) in a nutshell is:

For the Son of man is come to seek and to save that which was lost.

—Luke 19:10 KJV

For the Son of Man came to seek and to save what was lost.

—Luke 19:10 NIV

For I delivered to you first of all that which I also received: that Christ died for our sins according to the Scriptures, and that He was buried, and that He rose again the third day according to the Scriptures.

—1 Corinthians 15:3–4 NKJV

For I delivered unto you first of all that which I also received, how that Christ died for our sins according to the scriptures; And that he was buried, and that he rose again the third day according to the scriptures:

—1 Corinthians 15:3–4 KJV

We are now ambassadors for Christ. An ambassador is defined as "a diplomatic official of the highest rank, sent by one sovereign or state to another." When we became Christians, we lost our earthly citizenship. We instantly became citizens of the kingdom of God. Specific instructions and guidance for carrying out kingdom work is found in the book of Matthew, chapters 5 through 7. Jesus' message is commonly referred to as his trial discourse—how to live a kingdom citizenship life! As ambassadors, we are in the world, but not of this world. We now must adhere to the standards of the kingdom to be successful witnesses. Our major assignment is clear: to be light and salt (*see chapter 1*). We cannot rely on the world system to carry out our kingdom instructions.

You should teach people whom you can trust the things you and many others have heard me say. Then they will be able to teach others. And a servant of the Lord must not quarrel but must be kind to everyone, a good teacher, and patient.

—2 Timothy 2:2 & 24 NCV

And the things that thou hast heard of me among many witnesses, the same commit thou to faithful men, who shall be able to teach others also. And the servant of the Lord must not strive; but be gentle unto all men, apt to teach, patient,

—2 Timothy 2:2 & 24 KJV

Now then we are ambassadors for Christ, as though God did beseech you by us: we pray you in Christ's stead, be ye reconciled to God.

—2 Corinthians 5:20 KJV

So we are Christ's ambassadors; God is making his appeal through us. We speak for Christ when we plead, "Come back to God!"

—2 Corinthians 5:20 NLT

Now therefore ye are no more strangers and foreigners, but fellow citizens with the saints, and of the household of God;

—Ephesians 2:19 KJV

Consequently, you are no longer foreigners and aliens, but fellow citizens with God's people and members of God's household.

—Ephesians 2:19 NIV

We are commanded to spread His message through the good works in our lives.

And he said unto them, Go ye into all the world, and preach the gospel to every creature.

—Mark 16:15 KJV

And He said to them, Go into all the world and preach and publish openly the good news (the Gospel) to every creature [of the whole human race].

—Mark 16:15 Amplified

Now that we have changed official residences, our fortress, or embassy, becomes our new residence. Embassy is a noun, which is defined as "the official headquarters of an ambassador; a mission headed by an ambassador." The significance of an embassy is real. When someone bothers an embassy, a war breaks out! When someone bothers you and I, God goes to battle on our behalf. As an ambassador, we love our country (the kingdom of God) and we now live in a foreign land. We must be committed to the cause.

There is no glory in an easy assignment. We need to be challenged. Jesus makes a way to God, we make a way to Jesus. The more time we spend with Christ, the more we become like Christ. How we behave reveals what we believe...

You are God's children whom he loves, so try to be like him.

—Ephesians 5:1 NCV

Be ye therefore followers of God, as dear children;

—Ephesians 5:1 KJV

...and how we act on God's Word reveals how we believe it, as delivered to us by Christ's eyewitnesses...

FORASMUCH as many have taken in hand to set forth in order a declaration of those things which are most surely believed among us, Even as they delivered them unto us, which from the beginning were eyewitnesses, and ministers of the word;

—Luke 1:1–2 KJV

SINCE [as is well known] many have undertaken to put in order and draw up a [thorough] narrative of the surely established deeds which have been accomplished and fulfilled in and among us, 2Exactly as they were handed down to us by those who from the [official] beginning [of Jesus' ministry] were eyewitnesses and ministers of the Word [that is, of the doctrine concerning the attainment through Christ of salvation in the kingdom of God.

—Luke 1:1–2 Amplified

What are you believing?

Is hell only a state of mind? Some years ago, there was an article entitled, "Whatever happened to Hell?" in a prominent Black magazine. In this article, the writers had taken a poll of the major Black religious leaders of the time, and the consensus was that hell was a state of mind, not a place. The majority said that hell is right here on earth, and that people make their own heaven or hell. They added that there was no such place as heaven, that heaven was a state of mind.[14]

NOTES:

_____

_____

_____

_____

THERE'S A LARGE AUDIENCE
OUT THERE

The world begins where your front yard ends. Things are moving quickly and the world population is expanding rapidly.

Think about how fast things are happening around us: It took radio thirty years to reach its first fifty million Americans. It took television thirteen years. After only six years, the World Wide Web had a hundred million users. The next wave is broadband technology, which can transmit every issue of *The New York Times* from the last one hundred years in just one second.[15]

The United Nations Population Fund has designated October 12 as the "Day of 6 Billion" to commemorate—but not celebrate—a milestone reached with astonishing speed. Demographers say it took until 1804 to arrive at one billion people and another 123 years, to 1927, to double. The global community grew to three billion in 1960, and that number has doubled in just four decades. Birthrates are stable or declining in some thirty-two countries containing twelve percent of the world population, among them the prosperous industrial nations of North America, Europe, and Asia. Some developing countries like Brazil, Mexico, and South Korea have seen population growth slow as a result of various factors, including economic growth, higher education, and family-planning programs. But in regions like the Indian subcontinent, with 1.27 billion people, and sub-Saharan Africa, with a population of 770 million, birthrates are increasing by 3.8 percent per year. India, which had 358 million people in 1950, recently spurted past the one billion mark. It is expected to overtake China's 1.25 billion to become the world's most populous country and reach 1.5 billion around the year 2037. The question is: "It isn't how many people can the Earth sustain, but what level of suffering and ecological destruction we are willing to tolerate?"[16]

Jesus' own ministry and teachings reflect a concern not only for the spiritual well-being of people, but for their social, physical, and material needs as well. God's word is an arrow that never misses its mark.

For the word of God is quick, and powerful, and sharper than any two-edged sword,
piercing even to the dividing asunder of soul and spirit, and of the joints and marrow,
and is a discerner of the thoughts and intents of the heart.

—Hebrews 4:12 KJV

For the word of God is living and active. Sharper than any double-edged sword, it
penetrates even to dividing soul and spirit, joints and marrow; it judges the thoughts and
attitudes of the heart.

—Hebrews 4:12 NIV

Not everyone who reads God's Word turns to Christ. Jesus made this clear in the parable of the sower in Luke 8:4–15 (see chapter one of this guide). We are to be sowers of God's Word, but we don't decide who will receive it. Our job is to scatter the seed.

*Every day I was with you teaching in the Temple, and you did not **arrest** me there. But all these things have happened to make the Scriptures come true.*

—Mark 14:40 NCV

*I was daily with you in the temple teaching, and ye took me not: **but the scriptures must** be fulfilled.*

—Mark 14:49 KJV

In my current profession, I teach lessons and prepare presentations for diverse audiences. I have also managed staffs that range in number from six to as many as twenty-one. In this capacity, I have learned that the key to assigning work and having it completed timely and accurately is directly attributed to how the message is communicated to the listener. True communication means that the listener has heard and understands my message. If you want to be successful in life, then teach. You have to love the advice that you give. However, you must be knowledgeable about this one fact: the best listeners only retain 10% of what they hear. The percentage increases as the instructor/presenter follows through with a demonstration of what has been heard. The percentage increases even higher if a personal experience is discussed as a part of the learning process. A breakdown on listening patterns is as follows:

- ✓ Ten percent of message retained—tell them without any visual stimulation
- ✓ Sixty percent of message retained—tell them and provide visual stimulation
- ✓ Ninety percent of message retained—tell them, show them, and share a personal experience with them.

NOTES:

_____

_____

_____

_____

STUDY QUESTIONS AND DISCUSSION

Chapter Four

1. Will you spread the good news of Jesus Christ to at least ten people this year, and each year, for the rest of your life?

    _____

    _____

    _____

2. God is dependent upon each of us to spread the good news of Jesus Christ in the earth. Can He depend on you to do your part?

    _____

    _____

    _____

3. The Prayer of Salvation is simple and available to everyone. Will you encourage someone with prayer? (Romans 10:9, 13)

    _____

    _____

    _____

4. What will you do today to help those who have a desire to know God?

    _____

    _____

    _____

5. As Christ's representative in the earth, are you an effective witness? (1 Corinthians 3:23 and 2 Corinthians 5:20)

    _____

    _____

    _____

Chapter Five

Stand Tall by Knowing your Covenant Rights and Benefits

The Old Testament of the scriptures established *the law,* that is, the Ten Commandments. Under the law, God pronounced his expectations for a Godly lifestyle, through Moses, to the people of that time. The New Testament of the scriptures, beginning with the book of Acts, establishes a new and revised last will and testament of the Lord Jesus Christ called *grace.* We have been redeemed from the curse of the law, and transferred from the power of darkness into His marvelous light (1 Peter 2:9). Grace is God's omnipotent power working on behalf of the believer and our "Bill of Rights" is expressly revealed in the book of Romans through the book of Jude.

This book of the law shall not depart out of thy mouth; but thou shalt meditate therein day and night, that thou mayest observe to do according to all that is written therein: for then thou shalt make thy way prosperous, and then thou shalt have good success.

—Joshua 1:8 KJV

Beloved, I wish above all things that thou mayest prosper and be in good health, even as thy soul prospereth.

—3 John 2 KJV

*T*o do the will of God, we glorify Him by standing tall in our covenant *rights,* through righteousness. At the conclusion of the Prayer of Salvation, there is a conversion from the old to the new (*a rebirth*). We are literally translated from the power of darkness (Satan's kingdom) into the marvelous light (Kingdom of God or the Body of Christ). This "re-connection" process has now placed us into a new family, which has built-in covenant rights and benefits. Old things have passed away and ALL things have become new. The re-connection with God is instantaneous, however, the renewing of our minds relative to our new life is a continual process.

This chapter describes the transfer process into God's marvelous light. To really know, through our covenant rights and benefits that we now enjoy as believers, there are three essential elements:

- ✓ Bill of Rights—national, state, and scriptural "bill of rights";
- ✓ Grace versus "The Law"—a comparison; and
- ✓ Eliminate the F-E-A-R—God has not given us the spirit of fear.

<u>Central Theme</u>: Take hold of your covenant rights and benefits as a believer (through righteousness)
<u>Keyword</u>: Rights (righteousness)

The word "righteousness" embodies all that God expects of His people.

"Righteousness" defined:
Sedeq (Old Testament)—is a noun. This word is derived from a Semitic root which occurs in Hebrew, Phoenician, and Aramaic with a juristic sense. In Phoenician and Old Aramaic it carries the sense of "loyalty" demonstrated by a king or priest as a servant of his own god. In these languages a form of the root is combined with other words or names, particularly with the name of deity, in royal names. In the Old Testament, we meet the name Melchizedek ("King of Righteousness").
Sedeq occurs 119 times in the Old Testament and is found mainly in poetic literature. Its first usage is found in Leviticus 19:15. It is a legal term signifying justice in conformity with the legal corpus ("the law"—Deuteronomy 16:20), the judicial process (Jeremiah 22:3), and the justice of the king as judge (1 Kings 10:9, Psalms 119:121, and Proverbs 8:15).
Dikaiosunē (New Testament)—is the "character" or "quality of being right or just." It was formerly spelled "rightwiseness," which clearly expresses the meaning. It is used to denote an attribute of God

(Romans 3:5), the context of which shows that "the righteousness of God" means essentially the same as His faithfulness, or truthfulness, that which is consistent with His own nature and promises.

BILL OF RIGHTS

What is a right? It is a noun which means "something to which a person is entitled, as by just claim or legal guarantee." How are rights claimed within the Kingdom of God?

The book of Deuteronomy, which means "second law," the fifth (last) book of Moses, was written before the birth of Jesus Christ. It is comprised of a series of farewell messages by Israel's 120-year-old leader. It is addressed to a new generation who is destined to possess the land of promise (Canaan) at the end of a forty-year journey in the wilderness. The book itself contains a significant amount of legal detail. The entire chapter 28 (all 68 verses) is devoted to God's promised blessings and curses as Moses attempts to remind this new generation of the importance of obedience if they are to learn from the sad example of their parents.

What is most unique and intriguing about the book of Deuteronomy is that we have more recorded of what Jesus Christ said and did in the last week of His life than in any other. When Jesus answered the devil's temptations with, *"It is written,"* he fetched all his quotations out of this book (see Matthew 4:4, 7, and 10). Although this is an Old Testament book, it is very relevant today concerning our obedience to God's Word.

In Deuteronomy 28:1–14 (KJV), the promised blessings include:

:1 *"Set thee on high above all nations of the earth"*

:2 *"Blessings shall come on thee, and overtake thee"*

:3 *"Blessed shalt thou be in the city, and blessed shalt thou be in the field."*

:4 *"Blessed shall be the fruit of thy body, and the fruit of thy ground"*

:5 *"Blessed shall be thy basket and thy store."*

:6 *"Blessed shalt thou be when thou comest in, and blessed shalt thou be when thou goest out."*

:7 *"The LORD shall cause thine enemies that rise up against thee to be smitten before thy face: they shall come out against thee one way, and flee before thee seven ways."*

:8 *"The LORD shall command the blessing upon thy storehouses, and in all that thou setteth thine hands unto;"*

:9 *"The LORD shall establish thee an holy people unto himself"*

:10 *"And all the people of the earth shall see that thou art called by the name of the LORD; and they shall be afraid of thee."*

:11 *"And the LORD shall make thee plenteous in goods"*

:12 *"The LORD shall open unto thee his good treasure...to bless all the work of thine hand: and thou shalt lend unto many nations, and thou shalt not borrow."*

:13 *"And the LORD shall make thee the head, and not the tail; and thou shalt be above only, and thou shalt not be beneath;"*

NOTES:

_____

_____

_____

_____

In Deuteronomy 28:15–68 (KJV), the promised curses include:

:16 *"Cursed shalt thou be in the city, and cursed shalt thou be in the field."*

:17 *"Cursed shall be thy basket and thy store."*

:18 *"Cursed shall be the fruit of thy body, and the fruit of thy land,"*

:19 *"Cursed shalt thou be when thou comest in, and cursed shalt thou be when goest out."*

:20 *"The LORD shall send upon thee cursing, vexation, and rebuke, in all that thou settest thine hand unto for to do, until thou be destroyed, and until thou perish quickly;"*

:21 *"The LORD shall make the pestilence cleave unto thee, until he have consumed thee from off the land, whither thou goest to possess it."*

:25 *"The LORD shall cause thee to be smitten before thine enemies: thou shalt go out one way against them, and flee seven ways before them:"*

:29 *"And thou shalt grope at noonday, as the blind gropeth in darkness, and thou shalt not prosper in thy ways: and thou shalt be only oppressed and spoiled evermore, and no man shall save thee."*

:32 *"Thy sons and thy daughters shall be given unto other people, and thine eyes shall look, and fail with longing for them all the day long: and there shall be no might in thine hand."*

:41 *"Thou shalt beget sons and daughters, but thou shalt not enjoy them; for they shall go into captivity."*

:43 *"The stranger that is within thee shall get up above thee very high; and thou shalt come down very low."*

:45 *"Moreover all these curses shall come upon thee, and shall pursue thee, and overtake thee, till thou be destroyed;"*

:59 *"Then the LORD will make thy plagues wonderful, and the plagues of thy seed, even great plagues, and of long continuance, and sore sicknesses, and of long continuance."*

:61 *"Also every sickness, and every plague, which is not written in the book of this law,"*

:66 *"And thy life shall hang in doubt before thee; and thou shalt fear day and night, and shalt have none assurance of thy life:"*

In verses 1 and 15, *"if"* is the operative word. It denotes a contract between us and God. "If" we chose to obey His Word, 14 of the 68 verses in chapter 28 will shower us with blessings. We have favor in the sight of God and man. Conversely, by choosing not to obey His Word, we are subject to some promised 54 curses. These curses are built-in and inseparable from His Word. God's Word does not return to Him void and He cannot lie. We, therefore, must never forget the benefits (rights) that belong to His children (us) through obedience to His Word.

> *All that I am, praise the LORD; everything in me, praise his holy name. My whole being, praise the LORD and do not forget all his kindnesses.*
>
> —Psalm 103:1–2 NCV

> *Bless the LORD, O my soul: and all that is within me, bless his holy name. Bless the Lord, O my soul, and forget not his benefits:*
>
> —Psalm 103:1–2 KJV

NOTES:

_____

_____

_____

_____

American Citizenship

Our nationality, citizenship, and sense of belonging are usually determined by birth. By the fact that we were born in the United States of America (U.S.), we are "Americans." We enjoy certain rights and benefits under the *Constitution of the United States*[17] as drafted and adopted by this country's forefathers in the seventeenth century. Further, the Ten amendments to the *U.S. Constitution*, known as the *"Bill of Rights,"* guarantee certain freedoms to American citizens in which the *U.S. Constitution* itself had been silent.

The United States "Bill of Rights"

During the debates on the adoption of the *U.S. Constitution*, its opponents charged that as drafted, it would open the way to tyranny by the central government. These opponents demanded a "bill of rights" that would spell out the immunities of individual citizens. Thus, several states asked for such amendments while other states ratified the *U.S. Constitution* with the understanding that the amendments would be offered.

On September 25, 1789, the First Congress of the U.S. proposed to the state legislatures twelve amendments that met the arguments most frequently advanced against it. Ironically, the first two were not ratified; however, articles three through twelve were and constitute what we know today as the "Bill of Rights"—the first ten amendments to the *U.S. Constitution*. A brief synopsis of the amendments to the *U.S. Constitution* (The "Bill of Rights") are as follows:

Article I	-	*Freedom of speech, religion, press, petition, and assembly*
Article II	-	*Right to bear arms and militia*
Article III	-	*Quartering of soldiers*
Article IV	-	*Warrants and searches*
Article V	-	*Individual debt and double jeopardy*
Article VI	-	*Speedy trial, witnesses, and accusations*
Article VII	-	*Right for a jury trial*
Article VIII	-	*Bail and fines*
Article IX	-	*Existence of other rights for the people*
Article X	-	*Power reserved to the states and people*

NOTES:

_____

_____

_____

_____

Christian Citizenship

As Christians, we also have covenant *"rights."* We have a right to:

- ✓ A relationship with God (Romans 5:1–2),
- ✓ Fellowship with God (1 Corinthians 1:9–10),
- ✓ Abundant life (John 10:10),
- ✓ The peace of God (John 16:33), and
- ✓ Live a successful Christian and natural life (3 John 2).

By faith in Jesus, we are born again. We are now citizens of the city of the living God, heavenly Jerusalem, and our names are registered in heaven (Hebrews 12:22–23). We have been translated from the power of darkness (our old ways) into His marvelous kingdom (by salvation) and we now have a new covenant (a legal and binding agreement) that contains all of the covenant rights and benefits that we are to enjoy.

> *[The Father] has delivered and drawn us to Himself out of the control and the dominion of darkness and has transferred us into the kingdom of the Son of His love.*
>
> —Colossians 1:13 Amplified

> *Who hath delivered us from the power of darkness, and hath translated us into the kingdom of his dear Son.*
>
> —Colossians 1:13 KJV

These rights and benefits are expressly written in the books of Romans through Jude (New Testament). The book of Romans, written by Paul, is placed first among the thirteen (13) epistles in the New Testament. This book explores the significance of the sacrificial death of our Lord Jesus Christ. Jude, last among the thirteen epistles, encourages us to have faith in God and to fight against our spiritual enemies regarding that faith. The book of Galatians, which is one of the thirteen epistles, is the Christian's "Declaration of Independence."

A giant step toward knowing, accepting, and walking confidently in our rights and benefits as Christians is to know *The Holy Bible* and to not be ashamed of the truth as it revealed through the Holy Spirit.

To an inheritance incorruptible, and undefiled, and that fadeth not away, reserved in heaven for you, who are kept by the power of God through faith unto salvation ready to be revealed in the last time.

—1 Peter 1:4–5 KJV

And we have a priceless inheritance—an inheritance that is kept in heaven for you, pure and undefiled, beyond the reach of change and decay. And through your faith, God is protecting you by his power until you receive this salvation, which is ready to be revealed on the last day for all to see.

—1 Peter 1:4–5 NLT

Whosoever therefore shall be ashamed of me and of my words in this adulterous and sinful generation; of him also shall the Son of man be ashamed, when he cometh in the glory of his Father with the holy angels.

—Mark 8:38 KJV

If anyone is ashamed of me and my message in these adulterous and sinful days, the Son of Man will be ashamed of that person when he returns in the glory of his Father with the holy angels.

—Mark 8:38 NLT

NOTES:

_____

_____

_____

_____

Think Big

In his book entitled, *Think Big: Unleashing Your Potential for Excellence*, Dr. Ben Carson sets forth a dynamic strategy on his self-tested concept that he entitles "Think Big." The term refers to our innate ability to achieve, and have, those things that most people only dream about but never accomplish. We are born to be productive and to raise the level of productivity of those within our sphere of influence: children, friends, family, co-workers, bosses, saints, and especially those who do not have a relationship with God through Jesus Christ. Through our productivity, God is glorified! Each of us has a right to do so. Dr. Carson's formula is found below:

T	=	TALENT	If you recognize your talent(s), and use them appropriately, you will rise to the top of your field
H	=	HONEST(Y)	If we live by the rule of honesty, we can go far down the road of achievement
I	=	INSIGHT	If we commit ourselves to giving our best, we will come out on top
N	=	NICE	If we are nice to others, they will respond to us in like kind
K	=	KNOWLEDGE	If we attempt to increase our knowledge in order to use it for human good, it will make a difference in us and in the world
B	=	BOOKS	If we commit to reading, thus increasing our knowledge, only God limits how far we can go in this world
I	=	IN-DEPTH KNOWLEDGE	If we develop in-depth knowledge, it will enable us to give our best to others
G	=	GOD[18]	If we acknowledge our need for God, he will help us.

A business school cannot teach common sense, creativity, or imagination. These are uncommon talents[19]. A proper thought process is the beginning of thinking big. It is a Christian's right to practice the positive traits (attributes) that are outlined by Dr. Carson.

NOTES:

_____

_____

_____

_____

Denying your Christian Rights

"How bad science can be hazardous to your health"[20] and *"Church admits to shortage of miracles"*[21] are two recent examples of where the believer's covenant rights and benefits are being questioned or outright denied. In the first article, it was predicted that the world would end on May 5, 2000, in a book entitled *Voodoo Science*. On that day, the earth, moon, sun, and five planets lined up in what was thought would lead to worldwide destruction. In the second article, by Ruth Gledhill, the Church of England published a report, *"A Time to Heal,"* which emphatically states that God rarely performs miracles these days. The report, a four hundred page analysis produced by a Church working party, describes the growing popularity of Christian healing centers and acknowledges the existence of a deep spiritual quest in society.

NOTES:

_____

_____

_____

_____

> ## *"GRACE" versus "THE LAW"*

All Christians must understand that there is a difference between grace (New Testament) and the law (Old Testament). This is fundamental knowledge for the Christian to live a successful natural life. Christ has freed the believer from bondage to the law (legalism) and to sin (license) and has placed him in a position of liberty. In his writings, Paul demonstrates over and over that law and grace are two contrary principles.

For the law was given by Moses, but grace and truth came by Jesus Christ.

—John 1:17 KJV

For the law was given through Moses; grace and truth came through Jesus Christ.

—John 1:17 NIV

The Word of God says that grace and the law cannot co-exist.

Tell me, ye that desire to be under the law, do ye not hear the law?
For it is written, that Abraham had two sons, the one by a bondmaid, the other by a freewoman.
But he who was of the bondwoman was born after the flesh; but he of the freewoman was by promise.
Which things are an allegory: for these are the two covenants; the one from the mount Si'-nai, which gendereth to bondage, which is A'-gar.
For this A'-gar is mount Si'-nai in Arabia, and answereth to Jerusalem which now is, and is in bondage with her children.
But Jerusalem which is above is free, which is the mother of us all.
For it is written, REJOICE, THOU BARREN THAT BEAREST NOT; BREAK FORTH AND CRY, THOU THAT TRAVAILEST NOT: FOR THE DESOLATE HATH MANY MORE CHILDREN THAN SHE WHICH HATH AN HUSBAND.
Now we, brethren, as Isaac was, are the children of promise. But as then he that was born after the flesh persecuted him that was born after the Spirit, even so it is now.
Nevertheless what saith the scripture? CAST OUT THE BONDWOMAN AND HER SON: FOR THE SON OF THE BONDWOMAN SHALL NOT BE HEIR WITH THE SON OF THE FREEWOMAN.
So then, brethren, we are not children of the bondwoman, but of the free.

—Galatians 4:21–31 KJV (emphasis added)

Some of you still want to be under the law. Tell me, do you know what the law says?

The Scriptures say that Abraham had two sons. The mother of one son was a slave woman, and the mother of the other son was a free woman.

Abraham's son from the slave woman was born in the normal human way. But the son from the free woman was born because of the promise God made to Abraham.

This story teaches something else: The two women are like the two agreements between God and his people. One agreement is the law that God made on Mount Sinai, and the people who are under this agreement are like slaves. The mother named Hagar is like that agreement.

She is like Mount Sinai in Arabia and is a picture of the earthly city of Jerusalem. This city and its people are slaves to the law.

But the heavenly Jerusalem, which is above, is like the free woman. She is our mother.

It is written in the Scriptures:"Be happy, Jerusalem. You are like a woman who never gave birth to children. Start singing and shout for joy. You never felt the pain of giving birth,but you will have more children than the woman who has a husband."—Isaiah 54:1

My brothers and sisters, you are God's children because of his promise, as Isaac was then.

The son who was born in the normal way treated the other son badly. It is the same today.

But what does the Scripture say? "Throw out the slave woman and her son. The son of the slave woman should not inherit anything. The son of the free woman should receive it all."

So, my brothers and sisters, we are not children of the slave woman, but of the free woman.

—Galatians 4:21–31 NCV

So if the Son liberates you [makes you free men], then you are really and unquestionably free.

—John 8:36 Amplified

If the Son therefore shall make you free, ye shall be free indeed.

—John 8:36 KJV

NOTES:

_____

_____

_____

_____

Grace

The word *grace* appears over 170 times in the Greek text. It is such a common word in the Greek language that it is used with far more meanings than can be represented by any one term in English. Primarily, the word *chàris* denotes pleasant exterior appearance; gracefulness; loveliness. A distinguishing characteristic dwells on the inside of the believer. God's grace is sufficient to meet our every need in the natural. Grace comprises all sufficiency to be productive because of Jesus. It is His omnipotent power working on behalf of the believer. Through His favor, there exists a relation of active power as evident in 1 Corinthians 15:10 where Paul writes, *"not I, but the grace of God which was with me"* labored more abundantly than they all. Grace is something that labors. In 2 Corinthians 12:9, Paul writes, *"My grace is sufficient for thee: for my strength is made perfect in weakness."*

Galations—The Christian's "Declaration of Independence"
(The "Magna Carta of Christian Liberty")

Through Jesus Christ, we are declared independent. Dependent upon God, yet independent from the world system that is controlled and managed by Satan. Grace declares that you and I are complete, established, able to endure, and anxiety-free in our relationship with God. By casting all of our cares and concerns on Him, we are free to live a moral and righteous life without fear of retribution from this unkind world.

> *But the God of all grace, who hath called us unto his eternal glory by Christ Jesus, after that ye have suffered a while, make you perfect, stablish, strengthen, settle you. To him be glory and dominion for ever and ever. A-men.*
>
> —1 Peter 5:10 KJV

> *And after you have suffered a little while, the God of all grace [Who imparts all blessing and favor], Who has called you to His [own] eternal glory in Christ Jesus, will Himself complete and make you what you ought to be, establish and ground you securely, and strengthen, and settle you.*
>
> —1 Peter 5:10 Amplified

The book of Galatians is an epistle of Paul the Apostle that is written to the churches of Galatia who have become content with their exercise of faith. They are displaying outwardly signs of works, which becomes a concern of Paul's. His letter to these churches is an attack against gradual turn from faith to works. He learns of their actions from a report that the Galatian churches were suddenly taken over by false teaching(s) of certain Judaizers. Paul's message to the Galatians is so important that he chose to write it himself in lieu of dictating words to a secretary as was his usual practice (chapter 6, verse 11).

In chapter 3, there is a clear explanation, with details, that the Holy Spirit is given by faith, not by works. In other words, there is nothing that you and I can do to "earn" this precious gift from our Heavenly Father.

> *And for this cause he is the mediator of the new testament, that by means of death, for the redemption of the transgressions that were under the first testament, they which are called might receive the promise of eternal inheritance. For where a testament is, there must also of necessity be the death of the testator. For a testament is of force after men are dead: otherwise it is of no strength at all while the testator liveth.*
>
> —Hebrews 9:15–17 KJV

For this reason Christ brings a new agreement from God to his people. Those who are called by God can now receive the blessings he has promised, blessings that will last forever. They can have those things because Christ died so that the people who lived under the first agreement could be set free from sin. When there is a will, it must be proven that the one who wrote that will is dead. A will means nothing while the person is alive; it can be used only after the person dies.

—Hebrews 9:15–17 NCV

That being justified by his grace, we should be made heirs according to the hope of eternal life.

—Titus 3:7 KJV

Because of his grace he declared us righteous and gave us confidence that we will inherit eternal life.

—Titus 3:7 NLT

Having predestinated us unto the adoption of children by Jesus Christ to himself, according to the good pleasure of his will,

—Ephesians 1:5 KJV

For He foreordained us (destined us, planned in love for us) to be adopted (revealed) as His own children through Jesus Christ, in accordance with the purpose of His will [because it pleased Him and was His kind intent]—

—Ephesians 1:5 Amplified

Consequently, you are no longer foreigners and aliens, but fellow citizens with God's people and members of God's household.

—Ephesians 2:19 NIV

Now therefore ye are no more strangers and foreigners, but fellow citizens with the saints, and of the household of God;

—Ephesians 2:19 KJV

And God is able to make all grace abound toward you; that ye, always having all sufficiency in all things, may abound to every good work:

—2 Corinthians 9:8 KJV

And God is able to make all grace abound to you, so that in all things at all times, having all that you need, you will abound in every good work.

—2 Corinthians 9:8 NIV

And all who depend on the Law [who are seeking to be justified by obedience to the Law of rituals] are under a curse and doomed to disappointment and destruction, for it is written in the Scriptures, Cursed (accursed, devoted to destruction, doomed to eternal punishment) be everyone who does not continue to abide (live and remain) by all the precepts and commands written in the book of the Law and to practice them.

Now it is evident that no person is justified (declared righteous and brought into right standing with God) through the Law, for the Scripture says, The man in right standing with God [the just, the righteous] shall live by and out of faith and he who through and by faith is declared righteous and in right standing with God shall live.

But the Law does not rest on faith [does not require faith, has nothing to do with faith], for it itself says, He who does them [the things prescribed by the Law] shall live by them [not by faith].

Christ purchased our freedom [redeeming us] from the curse (doom) of the Law [and its condemnation] by [Himself] becoming a curse for us, for it is written [in the Scriptures], Cursed is everyone who hangs on a tree (is crucified);

To the end that through [their receiving] Christ Jesus, the blessing [promised] to Abraham might come upon the Gentiles, so that we through faith might [all] receive [the realization of] the promise of the [Holy] Spirit.

—Galatians 3:10–14 Amplified

For as many as are of the works of the law are under the curse: for it is written, CURSED IS EVERY ONE THAT CONTINUETH NOT IN ALL THINGS WHICH ARE WRITTEN IN THE BOOK OF THE LAW TO DO THEM. But that no man is justified by the law in the sight of God, it is evident: for, The just shall live by faith. Christ hath redeemed us from the curse of the law, being made a curse for us: for it is written, Cursed is every one that hangeth on a tree: That the blessing of Abraham might come on the Gentiles through Jesus Christ; that we might receive the promise of the Spirit through faith.

—Galatians 3:10–14 KJV (emphasis added)

NOTES:

_____

_____

_____

_____

The Law

The law was a standard of righteousness which we can be judged. The standard was obedience. "Law" is derived from the Hebrew word *nómos* which means "to divide," "distribute," "apportion," and generally meant anything established, anything received by usage, a custom, usage, or law. God knew that it would be impossible for man to fully obey the law, but it did serve as a rule laid down for guidance.

The Ten Commandments (Exodus, chapter 20) are commonly referred to as the law. Scripturally, the Ten Commandments are a reflection, or summary, of the first five books of *The Holy Bible*. They were laws given by God as guidelines for daily living, which are still relevant today. These laws are also known as the *Decalogue,* from the Hebrew word meaning "ten words." They are divided into two sections and can be summarized as follows:

✓ Our relationship to God (first four commandments)

1.   Trust God only (verses 3 and 4),
2.   Worship God only (verses 5 and 6),
3.   Use God's name in ways that honor Him (verse 7), and
4.   Rest on the Sabbath day and think about God (verses 8 through 11).

✓ Our relationship to other people (commandments five through ten)

5.   Respect and obey your parents (verse 12),
6.   Protect and respect all human life (verse 13),
7.   Be true to your husband or wife (verse 14),
8.   Do not take what belongs to others (verse 15),
9.   Do not lie about others (verse 16), and
10. Be satisfied with what you have (verse 17).

Jesus fulfilled the moral law by obeying, by bringing out its fullness of meaning, by showing its intense spirituality, and He established it on a surer basis than ever as the eternal law of righteousness. He fulfilled the ceremonial and typical law, not only by conforming to its requirements, but by realizing its spiritual significance. He lived them and although tempted to deviate from the law, He did not. Jesus did not commit any sin during His earthly ministry. He became sin, while on the cross, but never committed sin although opportunities were available for Him to do so. Jesus is our example!

Think not that I am come to destroy the law, or the prophets: I am not come to destroy, but to fulfil.

—Matthew 5:17 KJV

Don't think that I have come to destroy the law of Moses or the teaching of the prophets. I have not come to destroy them but to bring about what they said.

—Matthew 5:17 NCV

Your justice is eternal, and your instructions are perfectly true.

—Psalm 119:142 NLT

Thy righteousness is an everlasting righteousness, and thy law is the truth.

—Psalm 119:142 KJV

Finally, the law is fulfilled in one word: LOVE.

For all the law is fulfilled in one word, even in this; Thou shalt love thy neighbour as thyself.

—Galatians 5:14 KJV

The entire law is summed up in a single command: "Love your neighbor as yourself."

—Galatians 5:14 NIV

NOTES:

_____

_____

_____

_____

ELIMINATE THE F-E-A-R

FEAR: Mental Enemy #1 (**F**alse **E**vidence **A**ppearing **R**eal)

Fear is the mind's worst enemy and it raises extreme havoc when we allow it to enter and dominate our thoughts. Even though 98% of the things we worry about never happen, it still has a way of dominating us when it gets out of control. While fear can come to us in any of hundreds of different forms, there appear to be eight major fears that humans allow themselves to suffer most from:

Table 5. Eight Major Human Fears

Fear of	Going crazy
Fear of	Failure
Fear of	Sickness
Fear of	Poverty
Fear of	Not being loved
Fear of	Loss of love
Fear of	Old age
Fear of	Death

The primary emotions generated by the Flight or Fight Response are anger (the emotional energy to fight) and *fear* (the emotional energy to flee). Contained within these two are most of the feelings that we generally associate with the word *negative*. Consider these lists:[22]

ANGER
hostility
resentment
guilt (anger at oneself)
rage
seething
depression
hurt (you're usually upset with
    someone else, or yourself, or both)

FEAR
terror
anxiety
timidity
shyness (a general fear of others)
withdrawal
reticence
apprehension
grieving (fear that you'll never love or be loved again)

God admonishes us to eliminate fear from our lives. In His Word, there are several scriptures that support our ability to cast away fear:

And in nothing terrified by your adversaries: which is to them an evident token of perdition, but to you of salvation, and that of God.

—Philippians 1:28 KJV

And do not [for a moment] be frightened or intimidated in anything by your opponents and adversaries, for such [constancy and fearlessness] will be a clear sign (proof and seal) to them of [their impending] destruction, but [a sure token and evidence] of your deliverance and salvation, and that from God.

—Philippians 1:28 Amplified

For God did not give us a spirit of timidity, but a spirit of power, of love and of self-discipline.

—2 Timothy 1:7 NIV

For God hath not given us the spirit of fear; but of power, and of love, and of a sound mind.

—2 Timothy 1:7 KJV

Give your worries to the Lord, and he will take care of you. He will never let good people down.

—Psalm 55:22 NCV

Cast thy burden upon the LORD, and he shall sustain thee: he shall never suffer the righteous to be moved.

—Psalm 55:22 KJV

Come unto me, all ye that labour and are heavy laden, and I will give you rest. Take my yoke upon you, and learn of me; for I am meek and lowly in heart: and ye shall find rest unto your souls. For my yoke is easy, and my burden is light.

—Matthew 11:28–30 KJV

Come to Me, all you who labor and are heavy laden, and I will give you rest. Take My yoke upon you and learn from Me, for I am gentle and lowly in heart, and you will find rest for your souls. For My yoke is easy and My burden is light.

—Matthew 11:28–30 NKJV

NOTES:

_____

_____

_____

_____

Depression

Each year, more than nineteen million Americans suffer from persistent feelings of hopelessness and despair. Only a fraction recognize those feelings as depression. The problem has become so widespread, that October 5 has been designated as National Depression Screening Day. This is a day that has been set aside for people who think that they may suffer from depression can visit any of three thousand sites to be screened. In 1999, ninety thousand people sought help at these sites and nearly 70% tested positive for depression. Sixty-five percent of those did seek immediate treatment. Untreated, hopelessness can lead to suicide. Approximately thirty-one thousand people do so each year in the U.S., two thousand of which are under the age of nineteen.

The good news, according to the goal of National Depression Screening Day, is that depression can be "treated." This treatment can help a person find new strength and hope. New drugs have been tested and psychotherapy, which focuses on talking about the problem, also helps. Still, up to 75% of suicidal individuals indicate to someone that they have given up.

Both fear and depression start in the mind. How we control our thoughts is key to avoiding the trap of these two strongholds. God is not glorified through fearful or depressed representatives. Through the Word of God, we have overcome worldly anxieties by power, love, and a sound mind.

NOTES:

_____

_____

_____

_____

STUDY QUESTIONS AND DISCUSSION

Chapter Five

1. Did you know that spiritual rebirth makes you right with God? (Romans 6:18; 22–23)

_____

_____

_____

2. God has given us a free will to make choices. Do you realize that you are empowered to make Godly choices? (Deuteronomy 30:19)

_____

_____

_____

3. You have a right to "pray your day." Are you praying each day? (Matthew 6: 5–8) For example, are you praying for:
   - God's hedge of protection,
   - Wisdom and knowledge,
   - Safe travel to and from your appointed destination,
   - Your local church,
   - Peace on earth, and
   - Your family?

_____

_____

_____

4. What you are afraid of? You no longer have the spirit of fear. (2 Timothy 1:7, Hebrews 13:6, and Lamentations 3:22)

_____

_____

_____

5. Do you really believe that God's grace is sufficient to meet your needs? (2 Corinthians 9:8 and 12:9)

_____

_____

_____

Chapter Six

Be a Blessing to Others

Service to others is key within the Kingdom of God. Jesus took on the role of a servant throughout his entire thirty-three years on earth, and in particular, three and one-half years during his earthly ministry. Humbling ourselves as children and not thinking more highly of ourselves than we ought (Romans 12:3), serve as key barometers in our respective ministries. Whatever office you hold within your local church, service to others is first and foremost the most important, and perhaps most misunderstood, aspect of the ministry.

These things also belong to the wise. It is not good to have respect of persons in judgment.

—Proverbs 24:23 KJV

But is shall not be so among you: but whosoever will be great among you, let him be your minister; And whosoever will be chief among you, let him be your servant: Even as the Son of man came not to be ministered unto, but to minister, and to give his life a ransom for many.

—Matthew 20: 26–28 KJV

*T*o do the will of God, He is glorified through our service; in particular, our daily service to others. As was demonstrated in chapter one in this guide, *Glorify God at all Times,* human beings—each of us—have more in common than we have differences. It is such a waste of precious time and energy to cause harm to others than it is to service others for the betterment of all mankind. We are made in the image and likeness of an omnipotent (all powerful) God. Our new attitude toward God, and our desire to understand His Word, compels us to do good, as Jesus Christ is our example.

In this chapter, God will reveal to us that Jesus was a servant to others during His earthly ministry. In doing so, he accomplished great works and left many examples for us to duplicate as His ambassadors. God demonstrates in four ways that we are blessed so that we will be a blessing to others:

- ✓ We serve God through service to others—Jesus himself was a servant,
- ✓ Put aside hatred and prejudice—prefer no one over another,
- ✓ Look at what Jesus did—more parables in detail, and
- ✓ What can we do to help? Additional resources for you to consider.

Central Theme: How to be a servant.
Keyword: Serve

"Serve" defined:
Abôdāh (Old Testament)—"work; labors; service." This noun appears 145 times in the Hebrew Old Testament, and the occurrences are concentrated in Numbers and Chronicles. It is first used in Genesis 29:27.

A more general meaning of this word is close to our English word, "work." "Labor" in the field (1 Chronicles 27:26), daily work from morning until evening (Psalms 104:23), and work in the linen industry (1 Chronicles 4:21) indicate a use with which we are familiar.

Ebed (also Old Testament)—means "servant." This noun appears over 750 times in the Old Testament and first appears in Genesis 9:25. It was used as a mark of humility and courtesy, as in Genesis 18:3, and is the mark of those called by God, as in Exodus 14:31.

Therapōn (New Testament)—is a term of dignity and freedom meaning "to serve, to heal, an attendant, servant." It was used of Moses in Hebrews 3:5.

WE SERVE GOD THROUGH
SERVICE TO OTHERS

To serve has a two-fold meaning:
1.   To minister to the needs of others, and
2.   To effect change toward Godly behavior.

And whosoever will be chief among you, let him be your servant: Even as the Son of man came not to be ministered unto, but to minister, and to give his life a ransom for many.

        —Matthew 20:27–28 KJV

The greatest among you will be your servant. For those who exalt themselves will be humbled, and those who humble themselves will be exalted.

        —Matthew 23:11–12 TNIV

But he that is greatest among you shall be your servant. And whosoever shall exalt himself shall be abased; and he that shall humble himself shall be exalted.

        —Matthew 23:11–12 KJV

Teach those who are rich in this world not to be proud and not to trust in their money, which is so unreliable. Their trust should be in God, who richly gives us all we need for our enjoyment. Tell them to use their money to do good. They should be rich in good works and generous to those in need, always being ready to share with others. By doing this they will be storing up their treasure as a good foundation for the future so that they may experience true life.

        —1 Timothy 6:17–19 NLT

Charge them that are rich in this world, that they be not highminded, nor trust in uncertain riches, but in the living God, who giveth us richly all things to enjoy; That they do good, that they be rich in good works, ready to distribute, willing to communicate; Laying up in store for themselves a good foundation against the time to come, that they may lay hold on eternal life.

        —1 Timothy 6:17–19 KJV

Owe no man any thing, but to love one another: for he that loveth another hath fulfilled the law.

        —Romans 13:8 KJV

Keep out of debt and owe no man anything, except to love one another; for he who loves his neighbor [who practices loving others] has fulfilled the Law [relating to one's fellowmen, meeting all its requirements].

—Romans 13:8 Amplified

And we have known and believed the love that God hath to us. God is love; and he that dwelleth in love dwelleth in God, and God in him.

—1 John 4:16 KJV

And so we know and rely on the love God has for us. God is love. Whoever lives in love lives in God, and God in him.

—1 John 4:16 NIV

"The Golden Rule" is an appropriate pattern of behavior for servants. It is a basic knowledge for Christians and non-Christians alike.

And just as you want men to do to you, you also do to them likewise.

—Luke 6:31 NKJV

And as ye would that men should do to you, do ye also to them likewise.

—Luke 6:31 KJV

Therefore all things whatsoever ye would that men should do to you, do ye even so to them: for this is the law and the prophets.

—Matthew 7:12 KJV

Do to others what you want them to do to you. This is the meaning of the law of Moses and the teaching of the prophets.

—Matthew 7:12 NCV

Of whom much is given, much is required...

His lord said unto him, Well done, thou good and faithful servant: thou hast been faithful over a few things, I will make thee ruler over many things: enter thou into the joy of thy lord.

—Matthew 25: 21 & 23 KJV

The master was full of praise. "Well done, my good and faithful servant. You have been faithful in handling this small amount, so now I will give you many more responsibilities. Let's celebrate together!" ...The master said, "Well done, my good and faithful servant. You have been faithful in handling this small amount, so now I will give you many more responsibilities. Let's celebrate together!"

—Matthew 25:21 & 23 NLT

But the servant who does not know what his master wants and does things that should be punished will be beaten with few blows. From everyone who has been given much, much will be demanded. And from the one trusted with much, much more will be expected.

—Luke 12:48 NCV

For unto whomsoever much is given, of him shall be much required: and to whom men have committed much, of him they will ask the more.

—Luke 12:48 KJV

"Great leaders never desire to lead but to serve."[23] The word servant is used 58 times in the New Testament. It means one who is devoted to another at the expense of his own interest. Leadership can be seen as responding to responsibility. Natural and spiritual leadership can never be self-generated but only experienced as a result of a personal relationship with the manufacturer—our creator (God).

NATURAL LEADERSHIP	SPIRITUAL LEADERSHIP
Self-confident	Confidence in God
Knows men	Also knows God
Makes own decisions	Seeks God's will
Ambitious	Self-effacing
Originates own methods	Follows God's methods
Enjoys commanding others	Enjoys serving others
Motivated by personal interest	Motivated by love
Independent	God-dependent

In her book, *Jesus CEO: Using Ancient Wisdom for Visionary Leadership*, the author introduces the Omega management style. This style incorporates and enhances the Alpha management style (masculine, authoritative use of power) and the Beta management style (feminine, cooperative use of power). In her book, the Omega management style is based upon three simple premises:

1. One person, Jesus, trained twelve human beings who went on to so influence the world that time itself is now recorded as being before (B.C.) or after (A.D.) His existence.

2. This person worked with a staff that was totally human and not divine...a staff that in spite of illiteracy, questionable backgrounds, fractious feelings, and momentary cowardice, went on to accomplish the tasks He trained them to do. They did this for one main reason—to be with him again.

3. His leadership style was intended to be put to use by any of us.[24]

NOTES:

_____

_____

_____

_____

PUT ASIDE HATRED
AND PREJUDICE

Beloved, thou doest faithfully whatsoever thou doest to the brethen, and to strangers;

—3 John 5 KJV

Dear friend, you are faithful in what you are doing for the brothers and sisters, even though they are strangers to you.

—3 John 5 TNIV

The clear teaching of the Bible is to "love the brethen and the stranger." Both live near and far. God loves all equally. God's love has no limits. Our love should also have no limits. Jesus taught that we should love everybody, even enemies.[25]

From one man he created all the nations throughout the whole earth. He decided beforehand when they should rise and fall, and he determined their boundaries.

—Acts 17:26 NLT

And hath made of one blood all nations of men for to dwell on all the face of the earth, and hath determined the times before appointed, and the bounds of their habitation;

—Acts 17:26 KJV

Clearly, the race problem in the United States still exists and is running rampant. So much so, that *The New York Times* newspaper ran a six-part, front-page feature story from June 10, 2000 through July 16, 2000, entitled, "How Race is Lived in America." More than twenty *Times* correspondents and photographers worked on the project, for up to a year, reporting from schools, playing fields, churches, movie sets, and other locations to depict life as it is actually lived by different races in America. The six-week-long series focused largely on the everyday lives of little-known individuals. This topic is still so sensitive and touched so many Americans that even the Public Broadcast Station (PBS) aired a discussion on the *Times'* piece during the Jim Lehrer Newshour. The series, which is not pegged to any specific news event, culminated on July 16 in a special edition of the *New York Times Sunday Magazine*.

In the book of Genesis, chapter 10, the families (sons) of Noah are Shem, Ham, and Japheth. Each family was strategically placed within their bounds of habitation by God. Throughout this chapter, God reveals that all men (and women), after the Great Flood, descended from one of the three sons of Noah. From Japheth, verses 1 through 5 specifically state that *"the isles of the Gentiles divided in their lands; every one after his tongue, after their families, in their nations."*

Now these are the generations of the sons of Noah, Shem, Ham, and Ja'-pheth: and unto them were the sons born after the flood.

—Genesis 10:1 KJV

This is the family history of Shem, Ham, and Japheth, the sons of Noah. After the flood these three men had sons.

—Genesis 10:1 NCV

After Noah was 500 years old, he became the father of Shem, Ham and Japheth.

—Genesis 5:32 NIV

And Noah was five hundred years old: and Noah begat Shem, Ham, and Ja'-pheth.

—Genesis 5:32 KJV

And the sons of Noah, that went forth of the ark, were Shem, and Ham, and Ja'-pheth: and Ham is the father of Canaan. These are the three sons of Noah: and of them was the whole earth overspread.

—Genesis 9:18–19 KJV

The sons of Noah who came out of the boat with their father were Shem, Ham, and Japheth. (Ham is the father of Canaan.) From these three sons of Noah came all the people who now populate the earth.

—Genesis 9:18–19 NLT

From Ham, the lands of Cush (Ethiopia), Miz'-ra-im (Egypt), Phut, and Canaan were established (verses 6 through 20) *"after their families, after their tongues, in their countries, and in their nations."*

From Shem, communities were established that extended from Mesha into Sephar, the mountain of the east (verses 21 through 31) *"after their families, after their tongues, in their lands, after their nations."*

God's Word is clear that *all* people and families came from the three sons of Noah. Generations and nations were established in the earth after these three men, all sons of one of God's most righteous servants *"and by these were the nations divided in the earth after the flood"* (Genesis 10:32).

NOTES:

_____

_____

_____

_____

LOOK AT WHAT JESUS DID

Many books can inform, but only *The Holy Bible* can transform. Likewise, man crowns success, but God crowns faithfulness!

> *For what we preach is not ourselves, but Jesus Christ as Lord, and ourselves as your servants for Jesus' sake.*
>
> —2 Corinthians 4:5 TNIV

> *For we preach not ourselves, but Christ Jesus the Lord; and ourselves your servants for Jesus' sake.*
>
> —2 Corinthians 4:5 KJV

Jesus is our example of how to bless others through service. God is glorified, Christians are edified, and non-Christians can be convinced to change. Convincing precedes conviction. In the Parable of the Good Samaritan, Jesus responds to "a certain lawyer" who asks the question, *"Who is my neighbor?"*

> *And Jesus answering said, A certain man went down from Jerusalem to Jericho, and fell among thieves, which stripped him of his raiment, and wounded him, and departed, leaving him half dead.*
>
> *And by chance there came down a certain priest that way: and when he saw him, he passed by on the other side.*
>
> *And likewise a Levite, when he was at the place, came and looked on him, and passed by on the other side.*
>
> *But a certain Sa-mar'-i-tan, as he journeyed, came where he was: and when he saw him, he had compassion on him,*
>
> *And went up to him, and bound up his wounds, pouring in oil and wine, and set him on his own beast, and brought him to an inn, and took care of him.*
>
> *And on the morrow when he departed, he took out two pence, and gave them to the host, and said unto him, Take care of him; and whatsoever thou spendest more, when I come again, I will repay thee.*
>
> *Which now of these three, thinkest thou, was neighbor unto him that fell among the thieves?*
>
> *And he said, He that shewed mercy on him. Then said Jesus unto him, Go, and do thou likewise.*
>
> —Luke 10:30–37 KJV

Jesus answered, "As a man was going down from Jerusalem to Jericho, some robbers attacked him. They tore off his clothes, beat him, and left him lying there, almost dead.

It happened that a priest was going down that road. When he saw the man, he walked by on the other side.

Next, a Levite came there, and after he went over and looked at the man, he walked by on the other side of the road.

Then a Samaritan traveling down the road came to where the hurt man was. When he saw the man, he felt very sorry for him.

The Samaritan went to him, poured olive oil and wine on his wounds, and bandaged them. Then he put the hurt man on his own donkey and took him to an inn where he cared for him.

The next day, the Samaritan brought out two coins, gave them to the innkeeper, and said, 'Take care of this man. If you spend more money on him, I will pay it back to you when I come again."

Then Jesus said, "Which one of these three men do you think was a neighbor to the man who was attacked by the robbers?"

The expert on the law answered, "The one who showed him mercy." Jesus said to him, "Then go and do what he did."

—Luke 10:30–37 NCV

The very clear message here is to serve others. Notice that the "certain Samaritan" gave personal attention to the wounded man. He bound up his wounds, brought him to an inn, and took care of him. He stayed overnight and gave him money. Jesus asks in this parable, which of the three—the Pastor, the member of the Pastor's congregation, or the Samaritan—was the true neighbor of the wounded man? And to the certain lawyer, Jesus admonishes him to *"Go, and do thou likewise."* Concern for people is key!

Jesus' mode of questioning and instruction is quite convincing. He leaves no doubt as to the moral of each parable. His insight challenges the mind and leaves little to no room to confuse His message.

NOTES:

_____

_____

_____

_____

"A Friend in Need"

Then, teaching them more about prayer, he used this story: "Suppose you went to a friend's house at midnight, wanting to borrow three loaves of bread. You say to him,
'A friend of mine has just arrived for a visit, and I have nothing for him to eat.'
And suppose he calls out from his bedroom, 'Don't bother me. The door is locked for the night, and my family and I are all in bed. I can't help you.'
But I tell you this—though he won't do it for friendship's sake, if you keep knocking long enough, he will get up and give you whatever you need because of your shameless persistence."

And so I tell you, keep on asking, and you will receive what you ask for. Keep on seeking, and you will find. Keep on knocking, and the door will be opened to you.

For everyone who asks, receives. Everyone who seeks, finds. And to everyone who knocks, the door will be opened.

—Luke 11:5–10 NLT

And he said unto them, Which of you shall have a friend, and shall go unto him at midnight, and say unto him, Friend, lend me three loaves;

For a friend of mine in his journey is come to me, and I have nothing to set before him?

And he from within shall answer and say, Trouble me not: the door is now shut, and my children are with me in bed; I cannot rise and give thee.

I say unto you, Though he will not rise and give him, because he is his friend, yet because of his importunity he will rise and give him as many as he needeth.

And I say unto you, Ask, and it shall be given you; seek, and ye shall find; knock, and it shall be opened unto you.

For every one that asketh receiveth; and he that seeketh findeth; and to him that knocketh it shall be opened.

—Luke 11:5–10 KJV

This parable is actually entitled, "Parable of a Persistent Friend." Jesus' message is clear: Even though it may be inconvenient or the timing may not be ideal, we have a responsibility to help our friends at all cost. In this parable, a need was communicated at midnight, during the sleeping hours while in the bed with the children. Nonetheless, when a knock on the door occurs, Jesus instructs us *"to rise and give him as many (loaves of bread) as he needeth."* Similarly, Jesus is communicating to us this message: *"Ask, and it shall be give you, seek, and ye shall find; knock, and it shall be opened unto you."* Through the example of the persistent friend, Jesus comforts you and I in the knowledge that God is always available to listen to our plea. He is open to help us through any and all situations in life. We must trust Him and obey His Word in order to fulfill the desire of our hearts.

NOTES:

_____

_____

_____

_____

"Faithful and Wise Steward"

And the Lord said, Who then is that faithful and wise steward, whom his lord shall make ruler over his household, to give them their portion of meat in due season?

Blessed is that servant, whom his LORD when he cometh shall find so doing.

Of a truth I say unto you, that he will make him ruler over all that he hath.

But and if that servant shall say in his heart, My lord delayeth his coming; and shall begin to beat the menservants and maidens, and to eat and drink, and to be drunken;

The LORD of that servant will come in a day when he looketh not for him, and at an hour when he is not aware, and will cut him in sunder, and will appoint him his portion with the unbelievers.

And that servant, which knew his LORD's will, and prepared not himself, neither did according to his will, shall be beaten with many stripes.

But he that knew not, and did commit things worthy of stripes, shall be beaten with few stripes. For unto whomsoever much is given, of him shall be much required: and to whom men have committed much, of him they will ask the more.

—Luke 12:42–48 KJV

And the Lord said, "Who then is that faithful and wise steward, whom his master will make ruler over his household, to give them their portion of food in due season?

Blessed is that servant whom his master will find so doing when he comes.

Truly, I say to you that he will make him ruler over all that he has.

But if that servant says in his heart, 'My master is delaying his coming,' and begins to beat the male and female servants, and to eat and drink and be drunk,

The master of that servant will come on a day when he is not looking for him, and at an hour when he is not aware, and will cut him in two and appoint him his portion with the unbelievers.

And that servant who knew his master's will, and did not prepare himself or do according to his will, shall be beaten with many stripes.

But he who did not know, yet committed things deserving of stripes, shall be beaten with few. For everyone to whom much is given, from him much will be required; and to whom much has been committed, of him they will ask the more."

—Luke 12:42–48 NKJV

Christians and non-Christians alike are familiar with this popular parable. The overriding theme is *"to whom much is given, much is required."* In other words, as God's blessings overflow in our lives, we have an obligation to humanity to express unconditional love and render service to improve the conditions around us. We *are* blessed so that we can be a blessing to others.

Christ paid a debt he didn't owe to cancel a debt we couldn't pay.

NOTES:

_____

_____

_____

_____

WHAT CAN WE DO TO HELP?

The following resources emphasize ***service*** to others which is an expectation of Christ's ambassadors. These organizations also exist to be a blessing to those in need. You can do your part by contacting any of these resources that are provided.

Shelter

Volunteer vacations—Habitat for Humanity runs short-term mission trips to 67 countries all over the world. They can be reached at 1 (800)-HABITAT (422-4828) or visit www.habitat.org. Costs vary between $1,300 and $2,500, plus some incidental costs. As Habitat for Humanity prepared to celebrate its twenty-fifth anniversary, it saw the completion of the hundred thousandth house, during the Jimmy Carter Work Project/Building on Faith Week in New York City. Their goal was to complete the next 100,000 houses by 2005, one-fifth the time it took to complete their first 100,000. *"The whole concept of Habitat for Humanity is linking people up with one another."*—Millard Fuller, Founder and President.

Food

Every 3.6 seconds someone dies of hunger. Seventy-five percent are children. Donate free food to www.thehungersite.com. In its latest study on hunger, the U.S. Department of Agriculture reports that more than 10% of Americans faced hunger last year or worried that their food would run out. Despite a booming economy, 17% of our nation's children, about 12 million, did not get enough to eat. Hardest hit were single mothers, as well as African-American and Hispanic citizens. The report says that 30% of all single mothers and their children went hungry or lived on the edge of hunger, as did 21% of African-Americans and 20.8% of Hispanics.

Blood

At one time or another, virtually all of the Red Cross's thirty-six Blood Services regions appeal for blood donations in local communities. All eligible donors may call 1 (800) GIVE-LIFE. Patients who need blood in emergency situations absolutely depend on a readily available supply. To donate blood, one must be healthy, at least 17 years old, and weigh 110 pounds or more.

Relief organizations:

Compassion International

A child development ministry, disciplining and mentoring children in twenty-two countries through one-to-one sponsorship and Christian training programs. The exceptional graduates continue in Compassion's Leadership Development Program, sharpening their distinct talents and abilities and influencing their nations, and even the world, for Jesus Christ. They can be reached at 1(800) 336-7676 or www.compassion.com.

Josh McDowell Ministry: Telling the World the Truth!

This ministry is a division of Campus Crusade for Christ International. A worldwide evangelistic organization committed to sharing God's truth through challenging youth programs and global missionary work. They can be reached at 1 (972) 907-1000, P.O. Box 13100, Dallas, TX, 75313, or www.josh.org.

The Bible League

Wants to insure access to scriptures for all that desire it. Translation efforts and Bible shipments into places of persecution mark dedication to truly spreading the Word. Their purpose statement reads as follows: "We are called by God to provide Scriptures and training worldwide, so that people prepared by the Holy Spirit will be brought into the fellowship of Christ and His Church." Since 1938, over 1.3 million people in sixty countries have been presented the Gospel and have accepted Jesus Christ through this ministry. Their seven-fold mission includes providing scripture in over 679 languages and the New Testament in 325 languages. They can be reached at 1 (866) 825-4636 or www.bibleleague.org.

NOTES:

_____

_____

_____

_____

Other Facts to Consider

Every year, the <u>United Nations' Human Development Report</u>[26] looks for a new way to measure the lives of people. The report burrows into the facts about what children eat, who goes to school, whether there is clean water to drink, how women share in the economy, or who does not get vaccination against diseases that go on killing even though they are preventable. The world's consumption bill is $24 trillion a year.

The Haves

The richest fifth of the world's people consume 86 percent of all goods and services while the poorest fifth consume just 1.3 percent. The richest fifth consume 45 percent of all meat and fish, 58 percent of all energy used, 84 percent of all paper, has 74 percent of all telephone lines, and owns 87 percent of all vehicles.

The Have Nots

Of the 4.4 billion people in developing countries, nearly three-fifths lack access to safe sewers, a third have no access to clean water, a quarter do not have adequate housing and a fifth have no access to modern health services of any kind.

The Ultra Rich

The three richest people in the world have assets that exceed the combined gross domestic product of the forty-eight least developed countries.

The Super Rich

The world's 225 richest individuals, of whom 60 are Americans with total assets of $311 billion, have a combined wealth of over $1 trillion—equal to the annual income of the poorest 47 percent of the entire world's population.

Forty Billion a Year

It is estimated that the additional cost of achieving and maintaining universal access to basic education for all, basic health care for all, reproductive health care for all women, adequate food for all, and clean water and safe sewers for all, is roughly $40 billion a year. That is less than four percent of the combined wealth of the 225 richest people in the world.

Natural Resources

Since 1970, the world's forests have declined from 4.4 square miles per 1,000 people to 2.8 square miles per 1,000 people. In addition, a quarter of the world's fish stock have been depleted or are in danger of being depleted and another 44 percent are being fished at their biological limit.

Cosmetics and Education
Americans spend $8 billion a year on cosmetics—$2 billion more than the estimated annual total needed to provide basic education for everyone in the world.

Wristwatches and Radios
Two-thirds of India's 90 million lowest income households live below the poverty line. However, more than 50 percent of these impoverished people own wristwatches, 41 percent own bicycles, 31 percent own radios, and 13 percent own fans.

Telephone Lines
Sweden and the U.S. have 681 and 626 telephone lines per 1,000 people, respectively. Afghanistan, Cambodia, Chan, and the Democratic Republic of the Congo have one line per 1,000 people.

AIDS
There are over 33 million people estimated to be living with HIV globally. Though the global percentage of adults living with HIV has leveled off, there were still 2.7 million new HIV infections in 2007. Though access to treatment has increased over the past ten years, "HIV remains a global health problem of unprecedented dimensions," according to the *Status of the Global HIV Epidemic—2008 Report on the Global AIDS Epidemic*, at UNAIDS.org.

Pet Food and Health
Americans and Europeans spend $17 billion a year on pet food. This is $4 billion more than the estimated annual additional total needed to provide basic health and nutrition for everyone in the world.

NOTES:

_____

_____

_____

_____

STUDY QUESTIONS AND DISCUSSION

Chapter Six

1. Did you know that service to others blesses *you*? (2 Corinthians 9: 12-15)

    _____

    _____

    _____

2. "It is more blessed to give than it is to receive," is found in what New Testament scripture?

    _____

    _____

    _____

3. Before the feast of the Passover, do you really understand why Jesus washed the feet of His disciples? (John 13:1-20)

    _____

    _____

    _____

4. With Jesus Christ as our example, who will you serve today? (1 Peter 2:21 and John 13:15)

    _____

    _____

    _____

5. If all nations were made from one blood, and if God frowns upon those that prefer one over another, will you pray for deliverance from your prejudice and bias against people who do not look like you? (Acts 17:26, Romans 2:11, and James 1:9)

    _____

    _____

    _____

AFTERTHOUGHTS

Let us hear the conclusion of the whole matter: Fear God, and keep his commandments: for this is the whole duty of man.

—Ecclesiastes 12:13 KJV

Till I come, give attendance to reading, to exhortation, to doctrine.

—1 Timothy 4:13 KJV

*T*he overriding theme of **Give God the Glory!** is to *glorify God in all that we do so that we will lead others to Christ.*

In the spirit of the central theme of this book, we have examined six specific areas to help us to *know God* <u>and</u> *do the will of God.* Each chapter is progressional in terms of preparing our mind(s), or attitude, relative to how awesome God really is and to fix our hearts for action. To this end, here is a recap of each chapter and its focus:

PART I—KNOW GOD *(mental or attitudinal)*

Chapter 1. Glorify God at all times—in all things

To know God is to *glorify* Him at all times. This chapter illustrates how God is glorified in four ways:

- ✓ The parables of Jesus—a look at Jesus' earthly example(s) relative to words, thoughts, and deeds;
- ✓ Our human body—which is wonderfully and marvelously made;
- ✓ Our lifestyle—distinctively different character traits from the world; and
- ✓ Our faith—the only way to please God.

NOTES:

_____

_____

_____

_____

Chapter 2. Recognize and acknowledge your "calling"

To know God is to glorify Him through recognition and acknowledgment of our *"calling."* This chapter illustrates how God is glorified in four ways:
- ✓ Our predetermined ordination—an examination of Jeremiah 1:4–5,
- ✓ Salvation—the new birth examined,
- ✓ Our attitude toward our calling—the key mental attribute toward success with God, and
- ✓ Time values—how we manage time.

NOTES:

_____

_____

_____

_____

Chapter 3. Know your spiritual gift(s)

To know God is to glorify Him through our gift(s). This chapter illustrates how God is glorified through the working of *gifts* and how they tie into the nine fruits of the Spirit.

- ✓ Functional gifts,
- ✓ Operational gifts,
- ✓ Perfecting gifts, and
- ✓ Fruit of the Spirit.

NOTES:

_____

_____

_____

_____

PART II—DO THE WILL OF GOD *(functional or action driven)*

Chapter 4. Spread the gospel by telling and leading others

To do the will of God, we glorify Him by *spreading the gospel* (good news). This chapter illustrates how to know God by doing His will in three ways:

- ✓ Personal relationships—an examination of the book of Romans,
- ✓ Ambassadors for Christ—how we should represent Christ on earth, and
- ✓ There's a large audience out there—everyone is your neighbor.

NOTES:

_____

_____

_____

_____

Chapter 5. Know your covenant rights and benefits—stand tall

To do the will of God, we glorify Him by standing tall in our covenant *rights,* through righteousness. This chapter illustrates how to know God through the covenant rights and benefits that we enjoy as believers, in three ways:

- ✓ Bill of Rights—national, state, and scriptural "bill of rights";
- ✓ Grace versus "The Law"—a comparison; and
- ✓ Eliminate the FEAR—God has not given us the spirit of fear.

NOTES:

_____

_____

_____

_____

Chapter 6. Become a servant—a blessing to others

By doing the will of God, He is glorified through our service. This chapter illustrates how to know God through our service to others in four ways:

- ✓ We serve God through service to others—Jesus himself was a servant,
- ✓ Put aside hatred and prejudice—prefer no one over another,
- ✓ Look at what Jesus did—more parables in detail, and
- ✓ What can we do to help? Additional resources for you to consider.

NOTES:

_____

_____

_____

_____

I will conclude with this passage of Scripture taken from *The Daily Word* on August 19, 2000[27], which reads as follows:

Our Awesome Responsibility

What activity, what confusion surrounds us day after day! And we ourselves are busily carrying out plans and projects. In the midst of all this, the Lord is also at work. He's building His church, extending His kingdom of grace, and love, moving history to its God-honoring goal.

In all of His activity, the Lord is seeking to bring people into a love relationship with Himself. But love can't be mechanically coerced. It must be freely offered from the heart. God doesn't get people to love Him by proclaiming ear-splitting messages as if He were using a supernatural loudspeaker. He doesn't dispatch angels to astound unbelievers all around the globe. He doesn't fill the sky with spectacular signs.

The Lord wants the free trust and grateful love of men, women, boys and girls. So He works through believers as we obey the Great Commission (Matthew 28:19–20) and build our lives on a relationship with Christ (1 Corinthians 3:11–23). It's through your life and mine, through our dedicated talents, through our personal witness and untied ministry that God is winning the trust and obedience of lost people everywhere.

What an honor to be God's co-laborers—and what a big responsibility to be faithful stewards! (1 Corinthians 4:2)—VCG

> *We know that millions haven't heard*
>
> *About God's only Son,*
>
> *So we must witness where we are*
>
> *And tell them one by one.*
>
> —Sper

We must go to sinners if we expect sinners to come to the Savior.

Your Afterthoughts:

_____

_____

_____

_____

CONCLUDING PRAYER

My prayer for this Study Guide, as well as for each and every reader of this book, is the following:

Heavenly Father, I come to You in the precious and matchless name of Jesus. I come to You in that name because Your Word says that name has been highly exalted above every name that is named. Father, I come in agreement with my original prayer for this Study Guide and book series, and I thank You for the wisdom, knowledge, and understanding that You have granted unto me during this journey in my life. I thank You for the ability to complete this Study Guide, whose purpose is to touch the lives of all who read, study, and use it as a valuable resource. I thank You for the blessed gift of writing, and for all of the patience, ideas, and thoughts associated with this gift. It is a blessing to be an heir to Your Kingdom and a joint-heir with Your only begotten son, Jesus Christ.

I thank You for each and every person that reads and studies this Guide. You birthed them into the earth for a divine purpose. Help them, through this Study Guide, to come to know and fulfill their purpose. Bless them Father at their specific area of need—natural, spiritual, financial, professional, social, or mental, and grant them the desire(s) of their heart(s). While reading and studying this Guide, I ask that You grant them wisdom, knowledge, and understanding relative to Your Word and that they be moved to live a successful Christian life, in Jesus' name. For those readers who do not know You, prick their hearts so that they will develop a desire to know You, to confess the Prayer of Salvation in accordance with your Word (Romans, chapter 10, verse 9), and to allow You to come into their heart(s). I ask for your blessings and anointing on this Study Guide and its distribution throughout the world. Please continue to use me as a willing earthen vessel to spread the gospel of Jesus Christ globally and to help those in need to win in life. I lift this prayer up to You Father, in the precious name of Jesus, whose I am and whom I serve. A-Men.

APPENDIX A

Scripture references from the Preface of Book #1:
Know God and Do the Will of God Concerning *Your* Life

I accepted Jesus Christ as my personal Lord and Savior in the spring of 1993 and have witnessed the truth of God's Word as written, and revealed, in *The Holy Bible*. The new millennium, year 2000, is my anniversary, of sorts, for it symbolizes seven (7) years as a Christian. The number seven represents *completion* according to the Word of God. The word *completion* is derived from the Greek word *suntele,* whose meaning is "of completing something," "of the fulfillment of things foretold," "of God, in finishing a work," "to end together, bring quite to an end," and "accomplish." I have selected the following nine (9) scriptures from both the Old Testament and New Testament to support this biblical truth. For each of these nine scripture references, further explanation is provided below:

- Seven attributes toward complete knowledge of God (2 Peter 1:5 – 7),
- Seven days and nights for God's creation (Genesis 1:3 through 2:3),
- Seven deacons appointed in the early church (Acts 6:3),
- Seven local churches in Asia Minor (Revelation 2 and 3),
- Seven times hotter in the fiery furnace (Daniel 3:19),
- Seven seals, trumpets, and vial judgments (Revelation 6, 8, and 16),
- Seven times daily did David praise God because of His righteous judgments (Psalm 119:164),
- Seven times shall a just man fall and rise again (Proverbs 24:16), and
- Seventy times seven shall we forgive our transgressors (Matthew 18:21–22).

The number **seven** is significant in the Scripture as discussed below.

1. Seven attributes toward complete knowledge of God

And beside this, giving all diligence, add to your faith virtue; and to virtue knowledge; And to knowledge temperance; and to temperance patience; and to patience godliness; And to godliness brotherly kindness; and to brotherly kindness charity.

—2 Peter 1:5–7 KJV

For this very reason, make every effort to add to your faith goodness; and to goodness, knowledge; and to knowledge, self-control; and to self-control, perseverance; and to perseverance, godliness; and to godliness, brotherly kindness; and to brotherly kindness, love.

—2 Peter 1:5–7 NIV

NOTES:

_____

_____

_____

_____

2. Seven days and nights for God's creation

Creation of the World (Genesis 1:3 through 2:3, KJV)
Day 1—God said, *"Let there be light and called the light Day and the darkness Night"* (verses 3–5),
Day 2—God said, *"Let there be a firmament in the midst of the waters and God called the firmament Heaven"* (verses 6–8),
Day 3—God said, *"Let the waters under the heaven be gathered together unto one place, and let the dry land appear"* Thus, the Earth and the seas were formed along with vegetation, herb yielding seed and fruit (verses 9–13),
Day 4—God said, *"Let there be lights in the firmament of the heaven to divide the day from the night...and seasons and the sun, moon, and stars"* (verses 14–19),
Day 5—God said, *"Let the waters bring forth abundantly the moving creature that hath life, and fowl that may fly above the earth... after their kind, and blessed them"* (verses 20–23),
Day 6—God said, *"Let the earth bring forth the living creature after his kind...and God said, Let us make man in our image, after our likeness: and let them have dominion over the fish of the sea, and over the fowl of the air, and over the cattle, and over all the earth, and over every creeping thing that creepeth upon the earth...And God blessed them, and God said unto them, Be fruitful, and multiply, and replenish the earth, and subdue it"* (verses 24–31).
Day 7—God rested from His work and blessed this day and sanctified it (Chapter 2, verse 1–2).

NOTES:

_____

_____

_____

_____

3. Seven deacons appointed in the early church

And in those days, when the number of the disciples was multiplied, there arose a murmuring of the Gre'-cians against the Hebrews, because their widows were neglected in the daily ministration.

Then the twelve called the multitude of the disciples unto them, and said, It is not reason that we should leave the word of God, and serve tables.

Wherefore, brethen, look ye out among you seven men of honest report, full of the Holy Ghost and wisdom, whom we may appoint over this business.

But we will give ourselves continually to prayer, and to the ministry of the word.

And the saying pleased the whole multitude: and they chose Stephen, a man full of faith and of the Holy Ghost, and Philip, and Proch'-o-rus, and Ni-ca'-nor, and Ti'-mon, and Par'-me-nas, and Nic'-o-las a proselyte of An'-ti-och:

Whom they set before the apostles: and when they had prayed, they laid their hands on them.

And the word of God increased; and the number of the disciples multiplied in Jerusalem greatly; and a great company of the priests were obedient to the faith.

—Acts 6:1–7 KJV

NOW ABOUT this time, when the number of the disciples was greatly increasing, complaint was made by the Hellenists (the Greek-speaking Jews) against the [native] Hebrews because their widows were being overlooked and neglected in the daily ministration (distribution of relief).

So the Twelve [apostles] convened the multitude of the disciples and said, It is not seemly or desirable or right that we should have to give up or neglect [preaching] the Word of God in order to attend to serving at tables and superintending the distribution of food.

Therefore select out from among yourselves, brethren, seven men of good and attested character and repute, full of the [Holy] Spirit and wisdom, whom we may assign to look after this business and duty.

But we will continue to devote ourselves steadfastly to prayer and the ministry of the Word.

And the suggestion pleased the whole assembly, and they selected Stephen, a man full of faith (a strong and welcome belief that Jesus is the Messiah) and full of and controlled by the Holy Spirit, and Philip, and Prochorus, and Nicanor, and Timon, and Parmenas, and Nicolaus, a proselyte (convert) from Antioch.

These they presented to the apostles, who after prayer laid their hands on them.

And the message of God kept on spreading, and the number of disciples multiplied greatly in Jerusalem; and [besides] a large number of the priests were obedient to the faith [in Jesus as the Messiah, through Whom is obtained eternal salvation in the kingdom of God].

—Acts 6:1–7 Amplified

NOTES:

_____

_____

_____

_____

4. Seven local churches in Asia Minor

Revelation 2 and 3 (KJV)

Messages to the seven local churches at Asia Minor:
Ephesus—*"thou hast left thy first love"*

Smyrna—*"I know thy works, and tribulation, and poverty, (but thou art rich) and I know the blasphemy of them which say they are Jews, and are not, but are the synagogue of Satan"*

Pergamos—*"But I have but a few things against thee, because thou hast there them that hold the doctrine of Ba'-laam, who taught Ba'-lac to cast a stumblingblock before the children of Israel"*

Thyatira—*"Notwithstanding I have a few things against thee, because thou sufferest that woman Jez'-e-bel, which calleth herself a prophetess, to teach and to seduce my servants to commit fornication, and to eat things sacrificed unto idols"*

Sardis—*"for I have not found thy works perfect before God"*

Philadelphia—*"for thou has little strength..."*

Laodicea—*"thou art neither cold nor hot: I would thou wert cold or hot. So then because thou art lukewarm, and neither cold not hot, I will spue thee out of my mouth."*

NOTES:

_____

_____

_____

_____

5. Seven times hotter in the fiery furnace

Then was Neb-u-chad-nez'-zar full of fury, and the form of his visage was changed against Sha'-drach, Me'-shach, and A-bed'-ne-go: therefore he spake, and commanded that they should heat the furnace one seven times more than it was wont to be heated.

—Daniel 3:19 KJV

Nebuchadnezzar was so furious with Shadrach, Meshach, and Abednego that his face became distorted with rage. He commanded that the furnace be heated seven times hotter than usual.

—Daniel 3:19 NLT

NOTES:

_____

_____

_____

_____

6. Seven seals, trumpets, and vial judgments

The Tribulation Period Begins with the opening of the First Seal

<u>Revelation 6</u>—A Description of the First through Sixth Seals

First Seal—White horse symbolizes the antichrist (verses 1–2)
Second Seal—Red horse symbolizes war (verses 3–4)
Third Seal—Black horse symbolizes famine (verses 5–6)
Fourth Seal—Pale horse symbolizes death (verses 7–8)
Fifth Seal—Souls at the alter symbolizes persecution of the church (verses 9–11)
Sixth Seal—A great and violent earthquake symbolizes destruction that completely changes the
    earth (verses 12–17)

<u>Revelation 8</u>—A Description of the Seventh Seal

The Seventh Seal is opened and releases the Seven Trumpet Judgments

Seventh (and final) Seal—A silence in heaven symbolizes an adjustment period (verse 1).
First Trumpet—One-third of all grass and trees are consumed by fire, mingled with blood (verses
    6–7).
Second Trumpet—One-third of all sea creatures die, one-third of the sea becomes blood, and
    one-third of all ships are destroyed (verses 8–9).
Third Trumpet—A great star called "Wormwood," meaning bitter substance, fell from heaven
    and poisoned one-third of all the river waters (verses 10–11).
Fourth Trumpet—A third part of the sun, stars, and moon was smitten causing the day to lose
    one-third of its light. A loud voice called down from heaven, "Woe, woe, woe", to the
    inhabitants of the earth warning of three more trumpet judgments to come (verses 12–13).

<u>Revelation 9</u>—Fifth and Sixth Trumpets

Fifth Trumpet—A star fell from heaven unto the earth and to him was given the key of the
    bottomless pit. It was opened and there arose smoke of a great furnace which darkened the
    air. From the smoke came locusts upon the earth and they were commanded to hurt all men,
    for five months, who do not have the seal of God in their foreheads. Their leader's name, in
    the Hebrew tongue, is A-bad'-don (verses 1–12).
Sixth Trumpet—The four angels which are bound in the river Eu-phra'-tes are loosed which are
    prepared to slay one-third of all mankind (verses 13–21).

<u>Revelation 11</u>—Seventh Trumpet

Seventh (and final) Trumpet—The twenty-four elders fell upon their faces and worshipped God.
    Great voices in heaven proclaimed "The Kingdoms of this world are become the Kingdoms
    of our Lord, and of His Christ; and He shall reign for ever and ever (verses 15–19)."

<u>Revelation 16</u>

First Vial—A noisome and grievous sore (verses 1–2)
Second Vial—The sea became the blood of a dead man (verse 3)

Third Vial—The rivers and fountains of waters became as blood and every living thing died in the sea (verses 4–7)

Fourth Vial—Men were scorched with great heat as this vial was poured out upon the sun (verses 8–9)

Fifth Vial—Spiritual darkness was cast (verses 10–11)

Sixth Vial—The Euphrates River was dried up (verses 12–16)

Seventh Vial—"It is done" came forth as a great voice and thunders and lightnings as well as a great earthquake came forth (verses 17–21)

NOTES:

_____

_____

_____

_____

7. Seven times daily did David praise God because of His righteous judgments

Seven times a day do I praise thee, because of thy righteous judgments.

—Psalm 119:164 KJV

Seven times a day I praise you for your righteous laws.

—Psalm 119:164 NIV

NOTES:

_____

_____

_____

_____

8. Seven times shall a just man fall and rise again

For a just man falleth seven times, and riseth up again: but the wicked shall fall into mischief.

—Proverbs 24:16 KJV

For a righteous man may fall seven times And rise again, But the wicked shall fall by calamity.

—Proverbs 24:16 NKJV

NOTES:

_____

_____

_____

_____

9. Seventy times seven shall we forgive our transgressors

    Then came Peter to him, and said, Lord, how oft shall my brother sin against me, and I forgive him? till seven times? Jesus saith unto him, I say not unto thee, Until seven times: but, Until seventy times seven.

    —Matthew 18:21–22 KJV.

    Then Peter came to Jesus and asked, "Lord, when my fellow believer sins against me, how many times must I forgive him? Should I forgive him as many as seven times?" Jesus answered, "I tell you, you must forgive him more than seven times. You must forgive him even if he wrongs you seventy times seven."

    —Matthew 18:21–22 NCV

NOTES:

_____

_____

_____

_____

APPENDIX B

Psalm 23

Psalm of the Divine Shepherd

A Psalm of David

The Lord is my shepherd; I shall not want.

He maketh me to lie down in green pastures: he leadeth me beside the still waters.

He restoreth my soul: he leadeth me in the paths of righteousness for his name's sake.

Yea, though I walk through the valley of the shadow of death, I will fear no evil: for thou art with me; thy rod and thy staff they comfort me.

Thou preparest a table before me in the presence of my enemies: thou anoinest my head with oil; my cup runneth over.

Surely goodness and mercy shall follow me all the days of my life: and I will dwell in the house of the LORD for ever.

—Psalm 23 KJV

The LORD is my shepherd; I have all that I need.

He lets me rest in green meadows; he leads me beside peaceful streams.

He renews my strength. He guides me along right paths, bringing honor to his name.

Even when I walk through the darkest valley, I will not be afraid, for you are close beside me. Your rod and your staff protect and comfort me.

You prepare a feast for me in the presence of my enemies. You honor me by anointing my head with oil. My cup overflows with blessings.

Surely your goodness and unfailing love will pursue me all the days of my life, and I will live in the house of the LORD forever.

—Psalm 23 NLT

APPENDIX C

The Fall of Jerusalem

1. Jeremiah 39

    The eighteen verses of this chapter describe three significant events during the fall of Jerusalem:
    Jerusalem falls (verses 1–10),
    Jeremiah is released from prison (verses 11–14), and
    Edeb-melech is rewarded (verses 15–18).

    NOTES:

    _____

    _____

    _____

    _____

2. Jeremiah 52—The Capture of Jerusalem

    The thirty-four verses of this chapter describe the actual fall of Jerusalem as follows:
    How Jerusalem was captured (verses 1–11),
    The destruction of Jerusalem (verses 12–23),
    The people's exile to Babylon (verses 24–30), and
    The liberation of Jehoiachin (verses 31–34).

    NOTES:

    _____

    _____

    _____

    _____

3. 2 Kings 25:2

    And the city was besieged unto the eleventh year of king Zed-e-ki'-ah.

4. 2 Chronicles 36:13–21—The Destruction of Jerusalem

And he also rebelled against king Neb-u-chad-nez'-zar, who had made him swear by God: but he stiffened his neck, and hardened his heart from turning unto the Lord God of Israel.

Moreover all the chief of the priests, and the people, transgressed very much after all the abominations of the heathen; and polluted the house of the Lord which he had hallowed in Jerusalem.

And the LORD God of their fathers sent to them by his messengers, rising up betimes, and sending; because he had compassion on his people, and on his dwelling place:

But they mocked the messengers of God, and despised his words, and misused his prophets, until the wrath of the LORD arose against his people, till there was no remedy.

Therefore he brought upon them the king of the Chal'-dees, who slew their young men with the sword in the house of their sanctuary, and had no compassion upon young man or maiden, old man, or him that stooped for age: he gave them all into his hand.

And all the vessels of the house of God, great and small, and the treasures of the house of the LORD, and the treasures of the king, and of his princes; all these he brought to Babylon.

And they burnt the house of God, and brake down the wall of Jerusalem, and burnt all the palaces thereof with fire, and destroyed all the goodly vessels thereof.

And them that had escaped from the sword carried he away to Babylon; where they were servants to him and his sons until the reign of the kingdom of Persia:

To fulfil the work of the LORD by the mouth of Jer-e-mi'-ah, until the land had enjoyed her sabbaths: for as long as she lay desolate she kept sabbath, to fulfil threescore and ten years.

—2 Chronicles 36:13–21 KJV

He also rebelled against King Nebuchadnezzar, who had made him take an oath in God's name. He became stiff-necked and hardened his heart and would not turn to the LORD, the God of Israel.

Furthermore, all the leaders of the priests and the people became more and more unfaithful, following all the detestable practices of the nations and defiling the temple of the LORD, which he had consecrated in Jerusalem.

The LORD, the God of their fathers, sent word to them through his messengers again and again, because he had pity on his people and on his dwelling place.

But they mocked God's messengers, despised his words and scoffed at his prophets until the wrath of the LORD was aroused against his people and there was no remedy.

He brought up against them the king of the Babylonians, who killed their young men with the sword in the sanctuary, and spared neither young man nor young woman, old man or aged. God handed all of them over to Nebuchadnezzar.

He carried to Babylon all the articles from the temple of God, both large and small, and the treasures of the LORD's temple and the treasures of the king and his officials.

They set fire to God's temple and broke down the wall of Jerusalem; they burned all the palaces and destroyed everything of value there.

He carried into exile to Babylon the remnant, who escaped from the sword, and they became servants to him and his sons until the kingdom of Persia came to power.

The land enjoyed its sabbath rests; all the time of its desolation it rested, until the seventy years were completed in fulfillment of the word of the LORD spoken by Jeremiah.

—2 Chronicles 36:13–21 NIV

NOTES:

_____

_____

_____

_____

SELECTED BIBLIOGRAPHY

I have listed here only those writings that have been of significant use in writing this Study Guide. This bibliography may not be an exhaustive listing of works I have consulted. It is representative of the work used to form my views and is provided here as a reference tool for readers who desire to engage in further study.

Benton, D.A. *How to Think Like a CEO: The 22 Vital Traits You Need to be the Person at the Top.* New York: Warner Books, Inc., 1996.

Burkett, Larry. *What Ever Happened to the American Dream?* Chicago: Moody Press, 1993.

Caldwell, KirbyJohn H. with Mark Seal. *The Gospel of Good Success.* New York: Simon and Schuster, 1999.

Carson, Ben, M.D. with Cecil Murphey. *Think Big: Unleashing Your Potential for Excellence.* New York: Harper Paperbacks, 1992.

Fletcher, Kingsley A., Dr. *Prayer and Fasting: Purpose, Preparation, Action, Results.* Shippensburg, PA: Destiny Image Publishers, Inc., 1995.

Habitat World newsletter

Helzel, Leo B. and Friends. *A Goal is a Dream without a Deadline.* McGraw-Hill, Inc., 1995.

Henry, Matthew. *Matthew Henry's Commentary.* Hendrickson Publishers, 1991.

Hoelscher, Ross Von. *How to Achieve Total Success: How to Use the Power of Creative Thought.* Escondido, CA: Profit Ideas, 1990.

The Holy Bible. The New Open Bible Study Edition, King James Version. Nashville: Thomas Nelson Publishers, 1990.

Jones, Laurie Beth. *Jesus CEO: Using Ancient Wisdom for Visionary Leadership.* New York: Hyperion, 1995.

Kindersley, Dorling. *The Human Body, An Illustrated Guide to Its Structure, Function, and Disorders.* New York: DK Publishing, Inc., 1995.

London Times newspaper

Munroe, Myles. *Becoming a Leader: Everyone Can Do It.* Bakersville, CA: Pneuma Life Publishing, 1993.

Munroe, Myles. *Understanding Your Potential: Discovering the Hidden You.* Shippensburg, PA: Destiny Image Publishers, 1991.

New York Times newspaper

Orr, James, M.A., D.D., General Editor. *The International Standard Bible Encyclopedia.* Hendrickson Publishers, 1939, 1956.

Our Daily Bread, For Personal and Family Devotions. RBC Ministries, 1998–2000.

Price, Frederick K.C., Ph.D. *Beware! The Lies of Satan.* Los Angeles, CA: FaithOne Publishing, 1995.

Purpose magazine

Random House Webster's Dictionary, Third Edition. New York: Ballantine Books, 1998.

Roger-John and McWilliams, Peter. *You Can't Afford the Luxury of a Negative Thought—The Life 101 Series.* Los Angeles, CA: Prelude Press, 1991.

Sinetar, Marsha. *To Build the Life You Want, Create the Work You Love: The Spiritual Dimension of Entrepreneuring.* New York: St. Martin's Press, 1995.

South Somerset Extra newspaper

Sunday Star Ledger newspaper

USA Today newspaper

U.S. News and World Report magazine

Vine, W.E., Unger, Merrill F., White, William Jr., *Vine's Complete Expository Dictionary of Old and New Testament Words.* Nashville: Thomas Nelson Publishers, 1984.

Washington Post newspaper

ABOUT THE AUTHOR

Kevin Wayne Johnson is the eldest son of Ernest and the late Adele Johnson, raised in Richmond, Virginia. He attended and graduated from the Richmond Public School system and Virginia Commonwealth University, earning a Bachelor of Science degree in Business Administration/ Management, with a minor in Economics and a Finance concentration.

Kevin is a 24-year veteran of the federal government and corporate America in the career field of contracting and procurement. During his 24-year career, he negotiated contracts for a myriad of products and services including information and wireless technology, major weapons systems, consultants, spare parts, construction, architecture and engineering, and training; and is a graduate of the *1995 Executive Potential Program*. Kevin's written work has been presented before international audiences. He has testified before the United States House of Representatives Committee on Small Business, and he prepared testimony that was presented before the District of Columbia Committee on Government Operations.

Kevin's true love is for God. He confessed Jesus Christ as his personal Lord and Savior on May 2, 1993, alongside his wife Gail. This spiritual transformation occurred slightly less than two months after their marriage on March 6, 1993. He and his wife were ordained into the Christian ministry as deacons in 2000, and Kevin is a 2002 graduate of the True Disciple Ministries Bible Institute, Somerville, New Jersey. He and his family are active members of Celebration Church, Columbia, Maryland serving in the Children's Church ministry, the maturity leadership team, the ministerial team, President of WIN (Bible) Institute, and National Secretary for the Church of God National Men's Ministry and annual Conference. He speaks frequently at the requests of pastors/church leaders across the United States, teaching the Word of God before diverse congregations and denominations. Kevin is on the faculty at six regional, national, international writer's conferences teaching on his specialty: *From Start to Finish for the First-Time Author*. He is an adjunct professor at the National Bible College and Seminary in Fort Washington, Maryland where he teaches *Youth Counseling* and *The Covenants of God.* Kevin also teaches diverse subjects at the Celebration Church WIN (Bible) Institute as one of its certified instructors through the Evangelical Training Association, Wheaton, Illinois.

Kevin currently lives in Clarksville, Maryland, with his wife, Gail, and three young sons, Kevin, Christopher, and Cameron. He is the author of the *nine-book*, nationally best selling, series entitled **Give God the Glory!** Kevin has earned twelve (12) literary and media awards, including *2007 Memphis Black Writer's Conference Author's Hall of Fame Award* and *2006 & 2007 Christian Publisher of the Year*, Book Expo America, African-American Pavilion, and has hosted his talk show—**Give God the Glory!**— on the Voice America Internet Talk Radio Network (www.voiceamerica.com) and Black TV Online (www.blacktvonline.com), during the 2004–2007 seasons, reaching 300,000+ viewers per broadcast. He attests everyday that God *uses ordinary people to accomplish extraordinary things!*

<u>To order additional copies of this Study Guide:</u>
Winner of twelve literary/media awards, 2001–2008

Give God the Glory! **Study Guide**

Know God and Do the Will of God Concerning <u>Your</u> Life

Book #6, © 2008
ISBN: 978-0-9705902-2-0
Price: $15.00
Pages: 154
Dimensions: 8.5" x 11"
Paperback

Name: _____
Address: _____
City: _____
State/ Zip Code: _____
E-mail: _____

Mail order form with check or money order to: *Writing for the Lord* Ministries, 6400 Shannon Court, Clarksville, MD 21029. Please add $3.00 for shipping and handling.

This book series is available everywhere that books are sold OR order here:

Give God the Glory!
Know God and Do the Will of God Concerning <u>Your</u> Life

Book #1, © 2001
Fifth Printing
ISBN: 978-0-9705902-0-6
Price: $10.99
Pages: 162
Dimensions: 5.5" x 8.5"
Paperback

Name: _____

Address: _____

City: _____

State/Zip Code: _____

E-mail: _____

Mail order form with check or money order to: *Writing for the Lord* Ministries, 6400 Shannon Court, Clarksville, MD 21029. Please add $3.00 for shipping and handling.

Give God the Glory!

Called to be Light in the Workplace

Book #2, © 2003
Second Printing
ISBN: 978-0-9705902-1-3
Price: $14.95
Pages: 187
Dimensions: 6" x 9"
Paperback

Name: _____
Address: _____
City: _____
State/Zip Code: _____
E-mail: _____

Mail order form with check or money order to: *Writing for the Lord* Ministries, 6400 Shannon Court, Clarksville, MD 21029. Please add $3.00 for shipping and handling.

Give God the Glory!
Let Your Light So Shine, a devotional/gift book

Book #3, © 2004
Third Printing
ISBN: 978-0-9752572-9-6
Price: $7.95
Pages: 54
Dimensions: 5.5" x 6.5"
Paperback

Name: _____

Address: _____

City: _____

State/Zip Code: _____

E-mail: _____

Mail order form with check or money order to: *Writing for the Lord* Ministries, 6400 Shannon Court, Clarksville, MD 21029. Please add $3.00 for shipping and handling.

Give God the Glory!
The Godly Family Life
Book #4, © 2005
Second Printing
ISBN: 978-0-9705902-3-7
Price: $13.00
Pages: 200
Dimensions: 6" x 9"
Paperback

Name: _____

Address: _____

City: _____

State/Zip Code: _____

E-mail: _____

Mail order form with check or money order to: *Writing for the Lord* Ministries, 6400 Shannon Court, Clarksville, MD 21029. Please add $3.00 for shipping and handling.

Give God the Glory!
Your Role in Your Family, a devotional/gift book

Book #5, © 2006
First Printing
ISBN: 978-0-9705902-4-4
Price: $7.95
Pages: 56
Dimensions: 5.5" x 6.5"
Paperback

Name: _____

Address: _____

City: _____

State/Zip Code: _____

E-mail: _____

Mail order form with check or money order to: *Writing for the Lord* Ministries, 6400 Shannon Court, Clarksville, MD 21029. Please add $3.00 for shipping and handling.

Other books featuring Kevin Wayne Johnson's writings:

Blended Families: An Anthology
© 2006
*2008 Christian Small Publishers Association Non-Fiction Book of the Year

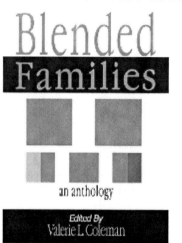

ISBN: 978-0-9786066-0-2
Price: $14.95
Paperback

The Secret: His Word Impacting Our Lives
© 2007

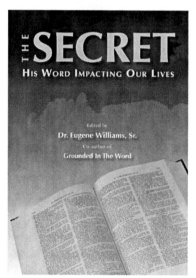

ISBN: 978-0-6151797-6-6
Price: $12.95
Paperback

To order, visit our online stores at: www.writingforthelord.com / www.writingforthelord.org

Now to Him Who is able to keep you without stumbling or slipping or falling, and to present [you] unblemished (blameless and faultless) before the presence of His glory in triumphant joy and exultation [with unspeakable, ecstatic delight]—To the one only God, our Savior through Jesus Christ our Lord, be glory (splendor), majesty, might and dominion, and power and authority, before all time and now and forever (unto all the ages of eternity). Amen (so be it).

—Jude 1:24–25 Amplified

Now unto him that is able to keep you from falling, and to present you faultless before the presence of his glory with exceeding joy, To the only wise God our Saviour, be glory and majesty, dominion and power, both now and ever. Amen

—Jude 1:24–25 KJV

NOTES

Chapter One

1 KirbyJohn H. Caldwell, with Mark Seal, *The Gospel of Good Success* (New York: Simon and Schuster, 1999), 29.

2 *The Daily Word* (1999).

3 "Timely Analysis of Key Developments in the New Economy," *Computer Economics eFlash,* (2000).

4 "Genetic Code of Human Life is Cracked by Scientists," *The New York Times* (2000).

5 Joannie Schrof Fischer, "We've only just begun: Gene map in hand, the hunt for proteins is on," *U.S. News and World Report* (2000): 47.

Chapter Two

6 "Samuel's Story," *Focus on the Family* newsletter (April 2000, Michael Clancy photograph of Samuel Alexander Armas care of SABA Press, New York, NY).

7 Russ Von Hoelscher, *How to Achieve Total Success* (Escondido, CA: Profit Ideas, 1990), 51.

8 Marsha Sinetar, *To Build the Life You Want, Create the Work You Love* (New York: St. Martin's Press, 1995), 85.

9 Leo B. Henzel and Friends, *A Goal is a Dream with a Deadline* (New York: McGraw-Hill, 1995), 8 (step #14).

10 Lyric Wallwork Winik, "There Must be More to Life," *Parade* magazine, (1999): 4-6.

Chapter Three

11 Dr. Kingsley A. Fletcher, *Prayer and Fasting: Purpose, Preparation, Action, Result,* (Shippensburg, PA: Destiny Image Publishers, 1992), 61-71.

12 D.A. Benton, *How to Think Like a CEO: The 22 Vital Traits You Need to be the Person at the Top* (New York: Warner Books, 1996), 397.

Chapter Four

13 Jim Davis, Melanie Diggs, and John Matney, "Roman's Gospel Message: The Good News of Jesus Christ," *Purpose* magazine (May 2000): 32.

14 Dr. Frederick K.C. Price, *Beware! The Lies of Satan* (Los Angeles: FaithOne Publishing, 1995), 23.

15 Quote by C. Michael Armstrong, AT&T Chief Executive, *Parade* magazine (June 11, 2000): 13.

16 "Global Population: 6 billion and counting, Little Morgan Luta arrives, unwanted," *U.S. News and World Report,* (1999): 46.

Chapter Five

17 The United States Constitution was adopted by a convention of states, September 17, 1787 and ratification was completed on June 21, 1788. To view the U.S. Constitution in complete detail, visit the website: www.law.emory.edu/FEDERAL/usconst.html.

18 Dr. Ben Carson with Cecil Murphey, *Think Big: Unleashing Your Potential for Excellence* (New York: Harper PaperBacks, 1992), 156-267.

19 Leo B. Henzel, 86 (step # 179).

20 Avery Comarow, "How bad science can be hazardous to your health," *U.S. News and World Report* (2000): 68.

21 "Church admits shortage of miracles," *The London Times* (2000): 13.

22 John-Rogers and Peter McWilliams, *You Can't Afford the Luxury of a Negative Thought—The Life 101 Series* (Los Angeles: Prelude Press, 1991), 35.

Chapter Six

23 Myles Munroe, *Becoming a Leader—Everyone can do it* (Bakersville, CA: Pneuma Life, 1993), 15 and 71.

24 Laurie Beth Jones, *Jesus CEO: Using Ancient Wisdom for Visionary Leadership* (New York: Hyperion, 1995), XVIII - XIV.

25 Quote by Millard Fuller, Founder and President of Habitat for Humanity International, in the *Habitat World* newsletter (October/November 2000), p.16.

26 "Kofi Annan's Astonishing Facts!" *The New York Times* (September 27, 1998), 16.

27 *The Daily Word*, RBC Ministries (August 19, 2000).

LaVergne, TN USA
28 September 2009
159250LV00002B/27/P